THE BUTTERFLY EFFECT

EFFECT

Healing is a Journey

*Names have been changed to protect the privacy of individuals

THE BUTTERFLY EFFECT

Healing is a Journey

DANIELLE CADOR

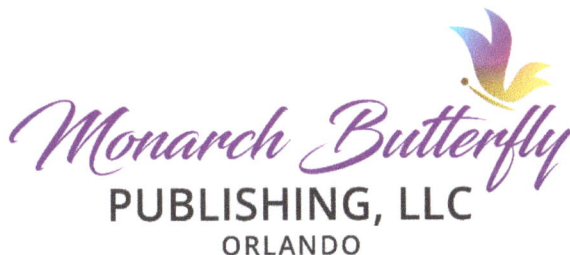

Monarch Butterfly
PUBLISHING, LLC
ORLANDO

Monarch Butterfly Publishing, LLC.
Orlando, Florida

www. monarchbutterflypublishing.wordpress.com

Printed in the United States of America

ISBN 978-0-578-67991-4 (Paperback) – ISBN 978-1-7351613-0-3 (Hardback) Non-fiction 1. Religion (Christian Ministry – Counseling & Recovery) 2. Christian Life (Inspirational)

Therefore if anyone is in Christ [that is, grafted in, joined to Him by faith in Him as Savior], *he* is a new creature [reborn and renewed by the Holy Spirit]; the old things [the previous moral and spiritual condition] have passed away. Behold, new things have come [because spiritual awakening brings a new life]. But all *these* things are from God, who reconciled us to Himself through Christ [making us acceptable to Him] and gave us the ministry of reconciliation] so that by our example we might bring others to Him]

2 Corinthians 5:17-18, AMP

Casting the whole of your care [all your anxieties, all your worries, all your concerns, once and for all] on Him, for He cares for you affectionately *and* cares about you watchfully. [Psalm 55:22.]

1 Peter 5:7, AMP

Contents

FOREWORD

On this journey that we call life there are things that will happen that will give us cause to stop take a deep breath and wonder why. It is at these times that we not only stop but we begin to ask ourselves the hard questions such as what could we have done differently. These stops, I like to refer to as threads in our tapestry of life. I encourage you to sit back and relax and consider the color of your threads as you read this very honest and humbling masterpiece as Danielle invites us in to witness her pathway to weaving just a corner of the tapestry of her life. Her threads will be familiar to some and inspiring to others. This is truly a journey worth taking. Your wings are waiting.

S. LaVerene Johnson

INTRODUCTION

Pain......ladies, we've experienced pain at some point in our lives, right? Giving birth to our children (that's a beautiful pain), a stubbed toe (whew.....those hurt), a broken friendship (or five), a breakup, loss of a loved one, and more. When a mother looks at her new born child, the pain of actually pushing this new human out of her body, begins to fade. She looks at this little person, with such wonder and amazement. The pain starts to subside, it lingers some (if not a bit more), but it eventually goes away. That stubbed toe, the one that took place in the middle of the night that pain begins to fade (even though that throbbing...whew....). A broken friendship, a breakup and a loss of a loved one, those pains can take a bit longer to heal. Healing....

Nobody wants to endure pain, any type of pain. I don't even want to experience a papercut (let's be real...that pain...whew)! Some of us will experience the type of pain that will tear at our minds, hearts, bodies and souls. The type that will hold us in bondage if we can't find a way to get the healing we need, or choose to hang onto that pain. Pain. Healing. Pain. Healing.

The story about a pain that lingered for a long time, is the one about the woman who was dealing with pain for 12 years. Some Bibles mention her as, 'The Woman with the Issue of Blood.' Now, I will be honest. When I first started studying The Bible and came across her story, I didn't really know exactly what the issue was. I knew she was bleeding, but no one could explain to me why she was bleeding. It always plagued me. Then, one day, I was reading the Book of Luke, and God opened my eyes to her story:

"And a woman who had [suffered from] a hemorrhage for twelve years [and had spent all her money on physicians], and could not be healed by anyone, and came up behind Him and touched the fringe of His outer robe. Jesus said, "Who touched Me?" While they were all denying it, Peter [and those who were with him] said, "Master, the people are crowding and pushing against You!" But Jesus said, "Someone did touch Me, because I was aware that power [to heal] had gone out of Me." When the woman saw that she had not escaped notice, she came up trembling and fell down before Him. She declared in the presence of all the people the reason why she had touched Him, and how she had been immediately healed. He said to her, "Daughter, your faith [your personal trust and confidence in Me] has made you well. Go in peace (untroubled, undisturbed well-being)."

-Luke 8:43-48, AMP
(Battlefield of the Mind Bible by Joyce Meyer)

It was brought to my attention that this woman was on her menstrual cycle, every day, for twelve years. TWELVE YEARS!!! Once a month can be a struggle, but every day.....for twelve years...with no signs of stopping....and much pain. She went to seek help from physicians, but they either couldn't or didn't want to help, but had no issue taking her money. No one could heal her. All of her money taken, but not healed, not even a little. "Heal....I just want to be healed," I am sure is going through her mind. All of a sudden, through a crowd of people, she sees Jesus. She's heard about Him. How He's healed people with a touch, a word, a prayer......she knows He can heal her. But, she's too far from Him. So, she reaches in between the crowd and touches His robe. She's mentioned in three of the Gospels. In Mark 5:28, it reads, "For she thought, 'If I just touch His clothing, I will get well.'" (AMP). Now, she's at the breaking point. She couldn't take the pain anymore, she spent all of her money on physicians, and they couldn't help, she heard about Jesus and by faith, she touched His garment, and she was instantly healed. She felt the healing power surge through her body. Blood was no longer just pouring out from her. Can you imagine? Blood just constantly pouring out from you, and people probably looking at you? Not wanting to be near you? She wanted the healing, and she pressed through to get that healing. Jesus felt the healing power leave Him, and wanted to know who touched Him. Jesus knew, but wanted that person to come up, step forward and admit that the person needed the healing. She knew Jesus noticed, so she confessed it was her. Jesus told her because of her **FAITH** and **CONFIDENCE** in Him, she was HEALED and to go live in peace.

The pain in the passage above was physical (body), mental (mind), internal, external, emotional and spiritual. Are you dealing with something like this? Jesus knows you need healing, the question is, do you know that you need healing? Are you able to admit that you've been holding onto pain for far too long, making it your safety net? Unknowingly, making it your cushion? Are you too afraid to let go of the pain because it has somehow become your identity? Or, are you willing to be like the woman with the issue of blood? Are you tired of going to someone who cannot help you? You've given everything you have to be healed, but you are still bleeding on the inside. There is One Who wants to heal you from all of your pains. One Who died on the cross to heal you of your hurts, gaping wounds and bleeding heart. What pain have you been holding onto? A rape? A sexual assault? A sexual harassment? A physical assault? Molestation?

Pain.....Healing.....Pain.....Healing.....Pain.....Healing.   It's   a journey. Not an easy journey. It's an ongoing journey. When that memory comes up, it's painful. Who wants to recollect a betrayal? An internal pain that just stabs at your soul? A painful tug at your heart? No one wants that. In the midst of your pain, hurts, tears and whys, can you hear Jesus whispering to you, "Come to Me, all *you* who labor and are heavy laden, and I will give you rest. Take My yoke upon you and learn from Me, for I am gentle and lowly in heart, and you will find rest for your souls. For My yoke *is* easy and My burden is light." **(Matthew 11:28-30, New King James Version (NKJV))**? His voice is really soft, calming, caring and loving.

Healing.....Healing.....Healing.....this is what Jesus wants for you. I promise, He wants to heal each part of you.

When Jesus looked at the woman, He didn't see her as 'the woman with the issue of blood,' He saw her.....HER. He saw her healed and so full of faith and confidence. When Jesus looks at us, He sees us....YOU!! Not the assault that took place. You're not the assault, you are loved. And, you are seen, heard and valued. This is what Jesus told me. This is how this journey began for me. Making a choice to heal instead of staying silent. The silence can be deafening, but it's time for you to be heard. It's time for me to be heard. To help encourage you to speak up, to remind you that Jesus loves you, and that you too, can begin your journey to healing.

HEALING IS A JOURNEY!!!

CHAPTER 1
THE MOVE:
On the Road Again

"I am a stranger in the earth; Do not hide Your commandments from me."

Psalm 119:19, New American Standard Bible (NASB)

W ho doesn't like to travel? See the world, not just the United States, but the world, be around different cultures, try different foods (not really my thing, but you get the picture), and learn a new language (Hola! Como esta? (come on Spanish), Sprichst du Deutsch (Hey German), or Ciao Bella! (whose Italian is not on point?). I definitely enjoy traveling. Primarily because my parents served in the military, so traveling was the way of life for my sister and me for years!! And, I did not complain about it. It may have seem burdensome to some...okay....to a lot of people, but being able to travel to another country (almost for free), where most people pay a lot of money to visit another country, you cannot beat that. I mean, The Philippines.......who just goes there to visit for a week or two? May I also add, one of my favorite places of the many we were stationed.

On the road again....that's a Willie Nelson song, right? I can hear it, the guitar, the notes, and....yes, Willie Nelson's voice (it came back to me). I was so used to living a life of moving every three to four years, to a new country (most of the time), or a new state. I was so used to being the 'new girl' in school, well, because that was the way of life for us. Again, no complaints from me. It was 'normal' to tell a friend, "Hey, once three or four years hit, I am going to be moving. But, we can still keep in touch by writing each other." (Hahahaha...this shows my age for sure. Do people even write letters to each other anymore? Is that a thing, or has it become a 'lost art?' I looked forward to receiving letters in the mail!!! Bills were not a thought at 12 years old. I just needed to know if I received a letter from Christy).

So, you could imagine my sadness.....maybe.....even disappointment when the time came for my mom to retire. Soooo...does this mean no more traveling the world? How does this retirement affect me? If I move afterwards, will I have to do it on my own.....and pay?! What is happening?! Of course, I knew this wouldn't happen forever, but I was feeling like I was somebody because of all of the places we had the privilege of visiting/staying. I mean, hop a flight to Okinawa for the weekend? Come on!!! Let me be honest, I had no idea how good I had it until my mom retired in 1995 (a year after I graduated High School). But, the big question....the eternal question....where is mom retiring?

COLORADO?!?! Are you serious?! You mean, where there's snow and mountains?! Are there any African Americans in Colorado? How long will this tour last? Oh, not a tour? Mom actually wants to retire in Colorado? Why? Because of the mountains? But, it's cold there. See, all of these questions came about within....an hour of our mom telling us that we would be moving to Colorado. Isn't it the horse state? We moved to Colorado in 1994 (after I graduated), and mom retired a year after that. I moved to Baton Rouge, LA to attend Southern University in 1995 (I took a year off after graduation and worked). Was not too pleased with the school, so in 2000, I moved back to Colorado......right.....the same place I was anxious to leave in the first place, but mom was there, and wherever mom is, that is home. I wanted to complete my education and get my Bachelor's Degree, so mom found a university in CO that would work for me in completing school. Spoke with a guidance counselor over the phone, and within minutes, my credits from Southern University were now being transferred over to Regis University (a Jesuit University and more for adults....accelerated program). In case you are wondering, Jesuit means to be a member of the Roman Catholic Society of Jesus (I am not Roman Catholic) and devoted to missionary and educational work. This was before I was saved, so I had no idea what Jesuit meant. To me, it sounded like a good place to complete my education.

After moving back to CO, I was able to get a job at a credit union. I pretty much had an on the spot interview (mom taught us to always dress up when looking for a job because you never know if they will hire you on the spot), and that is basically what happened. I've never worked for a credit union before, so this was definitely new for me. So much training in how to handle other people's money. Why is there a test? And, would you believe that the university was right next to my job? Like, literally, five minutes away!! I did mention in the actual interview that I would be attending Regis University, so the Area Manager (he was one of the interviewers) made that happen (we can say God did, but I didn't know this at the time). I GOT HIRED!!! I am going to be a bank teller. This should be exciting, being on the other side, getting to see how it all works out....you know, cashier checks, money orders, ordering checks (do people do that anymore?), and much more. This is like a brand new world. I feel like......an adult.

I will tell you, there was a lot to learn. Did I mention that there were tests? A lot of training....I mean a lot............which codes to use when depositing money into an account, which codes to use when withdrawing money from an account (if it's a business account....completely unique codes to use.....insert wide eyes emoji), a different code for transferring funds from one account to another, oh, don't forget to write down how much was given to you (the teller), or to the member (3x$20, 2x$10 and 4x$5 = $100.....did you get that?), and please don't forget to write your teller number on each transaction (in case there are any questions, or a member complaint, or a member compliment). Yes, so much to take in and remember. But, I will have to say, the branch where I worked was very accommodating to my school schedule. Classes were either from 530-730 PM (Mondays and Wednesdays) or 600-900 PM (Tuesdays and Thursdays). I didn't realize it then, but God really had that work in my favor (even then, before giving my life over to Christ, I was being looked after). Isn't that something?

Now, let me tell you, I had a mouth back then....like....a mouth. I see now that God was working on His daughter...like, really working. I pretty much had no problem letting people know how I felt about them (verbally or non-verbally). Oh, did I mention that Colorado has an Air Force Base? No? Well, they do, and some of the Generals, Colonels, Captains, you name it, would come in to handle a transaction, but with so much.....cockiness. I am all about respect, but it needed to go both ways. So, I did get some complaints about my attitude and demeanor. Can I tell you, your girl was a work in progress and didn't even know it! **Philippians 1:6** reads, **"And I am convinced *and* sure of this very thing, that He Who began a good work in you will continue until the day of Jesus Christ [right up to the time of His return], developing [that good work] *and* perfecting *and* bringing it to full completion in you."** (AMPC). Now again, I was not saved, but I could always feel as if God's hands were just on me. Like, He was saving me, and going to use me....but wasn't sure of what and how. Strange, I know, but it is true.

A little background about me and the church. I went to church when I was young. You know, when your parent(s) make you go to church, after you've been up all Saturday night/Sunday morning watching Saturday Night Live (remember when it had Eddie Murphy, John Belushi, Dan Akroyd, Chris Farley, Mike Myers, Dana Carvey, Steve Martin, Jane Curtin, Gilda Radner......showing my age again) and any old show that would come on? So, you go to bed around 130-200 in the morning. Then, your mom/dad (more than likely your mom) would come into your room around 830 Sunday morning to wake you up and say, "Get up! We're going to church." Like, you couldn't tell us that before we stayed up late watching TV? And, once at church, you better not fall asleep. Did you ever do that? No? Just me and my sister? (I am not ashamed to admit I did that). Okay, well there was no falling asleep during church. And, I am pretty sure, God gives all moms super powers (eyes in the back of their heads, sonic hearing, super speed......) because if we nodded off, and jolted back up, our mom was looking at us.....no.....more like.....glaring at us (insert wide eye emoji here). And, she would mouth, "You better not be sleeping in church." But, I am tired, and you didn't tell us that were coming to church today. I would've went to bed earlier (like, right after Saturday Night Live). Didn't really listen to what the pastor was saying (has it been two hours since he started preaching, or is that just my imagination? How much longer will this be going on? And, why does he keep saying that we'll leave when the good Lord tells us? Didn't he hear the Lord tell him we were done over an hour ago? I'm pretty sure I heard the Lord tell us that). But, as soon as the choir started singing, we knew it was time to get ready to go home!! Yes!!!! I think we were in there for about 4 hours. Pretty sure that's how long we were in there. Can someone explain to me why we were in there for 4 hours? I have questions that need answers.

As time went on, and I got older, I wasn't going to church as much. I had a Bible, but didn't really open it. I knew of God, heard of Jesus, and who is this Holy Ghost? What's his role in all of this? I thought it was just God? At my High School Graduation I was given a Bible. The good ole' King James Version (the thees and thous and hast and what the what?) I'll be honest, I took it with me when I moved to Louisiana for college. My grandmother (I was staying with her at the time) would go to church, but I went sparingly. My grandmother would tell me, "Your mom went to this church, so it's your church." I didn't agree with that because I knew that I needed to know God for myself. I wasn't all that interested, but I had the Bible, so I should be good. I think I went to church with grandma.....maybe....5 times the entire time I was living in the Bayou. I mean, if I could sleep in for a bit on Sunday because I could, I was going to.

Stay curled up in that bed. But, here's a kicker, I figured that if I wanted to learn some of the Bible, at night, I would put it under my pillow and the words would just sink into my mind while I was sleeping. Crazy huh? Well, I did that for the five years I lived at my grandmother's. I had a chapter bookmarked...Psalm 23. Why that chapter, I have no idea. That was the only scripture I knew. I also didn't know at the time that I was dealing with anxiety and depression, but for some reason, that chapter would calm me down. When I was feeling anxious or stressed, I would quickly go to Psalm 23 and read it over and over (I didn't know about Philippians 4:6. Hadn't made it there yet). This passage would give me peace,

The LORD is my shepherd; I shall not want.
He maketh me to lie down in green pastures: he leadeth me beside the still waters.
He restoreth my soul: he leadeth me in the paths of righteousness for his name's sake. "Yea, though I walk through the valley of death, I will fear no evil: for thou art with me; thy rod and thy staff they comfort me.
Thou preparedst a table before me in the presence of my enemies: thou anointest my head with oil: my cup runneth over.
Surely goodness and mercy shall follow me all the days of my life: and I will dwell in the house of the LORD for ever." (Psalm 23 King James Version (KJV))

That was my go to. I figured I was good strictly because I had that scripture memorized (basically, tattooed on my heart without even knowing it). Hmmm....it's amazing to see how God works in our lives, even when we don't know Him. He knows us. Wow!!! I can say that this was the beginning of me starting to tune in, even just a little, to God.

6

Back to Colorado........so, as I mentioned, I had a mouth. It did get me into trouble at times while working for the credit union during my early years. I was barely called into the principal's office in school (once for skipping), but while at the credit union......what was happening? It was like this rebellious spirit just jumped on me. I will admit, I didn't like it, but then.....I liked it, if you know what I mean. Not the being mean to people, but speaking up (could've done it in a better way, but......). We know, or at least we should know, that God can use our flaws to bring Him glory. Now, you are thinking, "If this young lady had a mouth, how is God going to use her?" Stay tuned (can I insert smirking emoji faces here? No, okay, then pretend you see smirking emoji faces here).

I was making great friends while at the location I was working at. Not far at all from the college I was attending, and my coworkers were very understandable about my schedule for school. Now, in Colorado, you know it snows. Like, snow, snow. That I had to get used to.

Driving up hills to and from work and/or school in the snow and ice. Definitely was not my testimony (or, the one I wanted at the time), but it was something I had to learn. Living overseas where it doesn't snow, or not as much, and then moving to a state where it is known for ski resorts......just wasn't my thing. I was doing well with my classes, and my behavior was improving at work. In May 2002, I completed my Bachelor's Program, and received my degree in Marketing/Management with a minor in Spanish. I wanted to pursue my Master's, but wanted to take time and not rush into it. So, I took the rest of the year to relax (was not missing writing papers, and studying for tests while working full-time). If I could, I would've traveled the world during this time, but 2002 was a year of moving out of my mom's and getting an apartment with a coworker (I was feeling grown), and working at a different branch. Not a bad thing, more growth within the credit union. To be honest, I got promoted quite a bit my first two years with the credit union. The positions I applied for, I got. I wanted to learn as much as possible, and not be limited.

Hello, 2003!!!! What do you have planned for me this year? How about..........YOUR FIRST BOYFRIEND?!?!?! Yes, you read that correctly. My first boyfriend at the age of 26 (soon to be 27). How can this be, you ask? In elementary school, I was too busy beating up boys (one made fun of the way said, 'ask.' It sounded like 'axe.' I punched him in his throat. Yes, yes, I know it was wrong, but don't make fun of me. I think he liked me, but I wasn't thinking about that in the 2nd grade). Then, in high school, I didn't date because I knew how the guys in my grade......actually, 7th-12th grade, behaved so I didn't want any part of that. They were not going to spread gossips about me. Although, me not being promiscuous seemed to intrigue the boys in school anyhow. But, I wasn't going to give in, so no boyfriend in high school. By college, I think I was afraid to date because of three things: 1.) I never dated before, 2.) I was living in Louisiana (new atmosphere) and 3.) I didn't want to become pregnant (quite a few of the girls that I became friends with at the beginning of my college years became pregnant within two years of us being at Southern University). And to be honest, I wasn't really looking to be in a relationship. But, this one came about. His name was *Eric. We met at work. I thought he was super cute. I would catch him looking at me, you know.....the sly look over, the admiring (I would hope was admiring). I mean, I made it a point to sometime pass the Teller line more than needed so that he would notice me. I remember telling a few friends about him. They made it a point to come over to the branch I was working at, and have lunch, just so they could see him. They agreed he was cute. Now, let me be honest with you, he was not my 'type.' I don't think I have a type, but he was one that I didn't see myself dating. Blonde hair, blue eyes, played football in high school and dressed like he an Abercrombie & Fitch model. No, definitely not my type. I mean, Abercrombie & Fitch (is that store still around, and wasn't that in a song at one point)? That's almost preppy, but high class, right? What song was this store mentioned in? If you remember, please let me know. I can hear it. Something about ...'New Kids on the Block had a bunch of hits, Chinese food makes me sick.' But, I was attracted to him. Now, that I think about it, he paid attention to me, he was cute, he thought I was hot, so.......why not fall for him....right?

After some flirting for a few months, he did ask me out (at the end of 2002). We became official in 2003!! That's still a big deal, right?! Becoming official with your boyfriend...exclusive?! Now, being that we worked at the same branch, we were keeping our relationship quiet. One of the reasons, for me, was that he was younger.......like.............more than 6 years younger than me. Don't ask. No, I was not trying to be a cougar. I had no idea how old he was until right before he asked me out. Then, I told him my age, and he didn't care. Maybe he liked the idea of being with an older woman. Anyhow, that was a main reason for me. Plus, I didn't want people in my business and talking about us. We would still talk at work, but kept it professional. We didn't go to lunch together. By the summer of 2003, I had my own apartment, so he was coming over regularly. I met his parents, and his mom took to me right away. She didn't care that her son was dating an older African American woman. She wanted us married soon....almost like....ASAP! His dad was never much of a talker, so I couldn't tell if he liked me at first (I found out later that he did). So, you know by him being younger, he still lived with his parents? I just wanted to make that clear. His mom didn't mind if he stayed the night at my place, or if I stayed the night over at their place. Now, with my mom, if I was staying with her, that wasn't happening. Actually, if she knew he was staying some nights at my place (she will now if she reads this book), she would've been disappointed in me. Would not have been the first time.

Six months into dating, and I am thinking he could be the one!!! We couldn't wait to see each other after work so that we could hold hands and kiss. Football season is starting, and I have a boyfriend who can tell me about football because he played it in high school (like a year or three prior....remember he's way younger than me). I learned a lot that year about football; who the players were (Brett Favre was with Green Bay, Steve McNair was with Tennessee, Peyton Manning was with Indy, Dante Hall was with the Chiefs, Adam Vinateri was with the Patriots, you get the idea). Eric and his dad shared a lot. I learned that we do not talk during the games (still a rule I go by), ask questions during commercials (still a rule I go by today), and that you need a team. So, my love affair with the Indianapolis Colts began. At first, I liked the Kansas City Chiefs, then, I watched the Colts play, and I was like, "Wait a minute. Marvin Harrison and Reggie Wayne are beasts on the field." I had no idea who Peyton Manning was because I was intrigued by the team atmosphere. After a game of the Chiefs playing the Colts (I was torn), I decided to be a full-time Colts fan! It was that team dynamic that was drawing me to them. And, I became a HUGE fan of the coach, Tony Dungy. He seemed so calm and collected. And, who is the Quarterback again? Ohhhhhh.....that's Peyton Manning.

Okay, he's not bad. Seems to be a good leader. The other players respect him. He respects Mr. Dungy. And, I like the colors blue and white, so this can definitely work. This was something that was bridging Eric and me closer to each other. It was a time for us to spend with each other, and watch America's favorite pastime. By the end of 2003 and the beginning of 2004, we had spent our first Christmas and New Year's together. I had a boyfriend during the holidays, you guys. Yes, I was excited!!

About to hit our 1 year anniversary of being a couple, so talk of getting married were starting to come up. His mom was pushing for us to get married too. But, I will be honest, I did want to get married. Thinking back, I didn't want to be in my late twenties not married. Isn't that the age to get married? When you're in your twenties? **Do not be conformed to this world (this age), [fashioned after and adapted to its external, superficial customs], but be transformed (changed) by the [entire] renewal of your mind [by its new ideals and its new attitude], so that you may prove [for yourselves] what is the good and acceptable and perfect will of God,** *even* **the thing which is good and acceptable and perfect [in His sight for you]. – Romans 12:2 AMPC.** Did you get that? We did talk about it at times, but I didn't want to bring it up because I was afraid that it would push him away, and I didn't want to do that. My mom had met Eric a few times. I could tell she wasn't impressed (he was younger and white). I remember his mom wanted to meet my mom, so she invited mom to dinner. The olive branch was out. Eric's mom actually invited my mom and sister, but my sister worked nights. Mom came over to the house, and had attitude. It broke my heart. Eric's mom went out of her way to make a great meal, and started up conversations, but mom wasn't budging much. She wasn't friendly. I wonder if Eric's mom could feel that. Will she look at me differently because how my mom is responding? That dinner was not how I imagined going. Thankfully, his mom was not too phased by mom's demeanor. I don't think we ever talk about it. Nonetheless, 2004 was ending pretty well. My friends like my boyfriend, we are getting along, we're talking marriage and both are working. Come on 2005!

Well, I thought this was going to be the year that Eric would propose. 2005 was going to be the year! Thank You, God! It seemed as if he was hinting around to it. For Easter, he did like the Easter egg hunt. I was thinking, this must be it!!! I'll find the egg, and the ring will be in there. I mean, it would be something different as far as proposals go (for me anyhow). That wasn't the case. He wanted to do something a little fun, plus, I mentioned that I never really did an Easter egg hunt, so this was his way of bringing that to life. It was cute......but, I was hoping for a proposal. I made sure to hide my disappointment.

I also started to notice little holes in our relationship......more like BIG holes. In the beginning of our relationship, we didn't argue. For real, no arguments (I guess that's not normal, or more, what we were talking about all this time for there not to be an argument). The one that sticks out the most (there are two) had to do with my jacket. You see, Eric bought me a nice suede jacket for Christmas 2004. I mean.....NICE!!! It came from Abercrombie & Fitch (his favorite store). He worked there part-time, so he had an employee discount. Because it was so nice, I didn't want to wear it like an everyday jacket (it had a nice hood with faux fur around it). Who wants to go to a seafood restaurant and have their jacket smell like seafood? Not me. Plus, there was an employee at my job that I was not fond of, so I didn't want her seeing my new jacket (petty, I know). Being that I would stay a few nights at a time over at his place (his parents, let's just call it what was), I would leave clothes over there. Well, one night, we were going to dinner and I wanted to wear my jacket. I looked in the closet......I don't see my jacket. I am searching all over (you know how you overlook an item because it was bunched up or hidden behind another item), still don't see it. So, I asked Eric if he'd seen my jacket. He told me that he took it back to the store. WHAT?!?!?! Why would you take it back? It's my jacket! He told me, "You don't wear the jacket. It hangs in the closet and you're making a BIG deal about not letting (we'll call her Katie) see the jacket." He got me there about Katie, I will be honest about that. But, I explained to him. "You had no right taking **MY** jacket back to the store. You bought it for me. It's my choice when to wear the jacket, and I don't want to wear it like an everyday jacket. It's suede. I want to take care of it and not get spots and dirt on it. That was **MY JACKET!!!** I bought you a men's bracelet for our year and a half anniversary, and you don't wear that. I don't make a BIG deal about it!" We argued a bit more, then I left. How could he do such a thing?! That was my jacket! **MINE!!!** I was so upset! We didn't talk for a couple of days. I will be honest, I really was not worried about it. You know how there are some arguments in a relationships/friendships, where you're like, "This is it. It's over." I didn't think this was the one that would end us. I was just upset, and I am sure he was too. After a couple of days, he called me to say he wanted to talk. I wasn't nervous. He asked if I could come over, I told him I couldn't (a lie), so he said he would come over to my place. He apologized for taking my jacket back to the store. He had a surprise for me......he got my jacket back. I wasn't expecting that. If he wasn't going to get it back, that was fine. I just wanted him to know how inconsiderate it was. We talked a bit more. That situation was settled. Thank You, God.

It's May 2005, and I am getting my Master's Degree!!! Woo hoo!!! It's a big deal because I am the first grandchild on my both sides and the first to go for their Master's Degree. It's time to celebrate!!! One of my friends threw me a BIG graduation dinner. I had family come into town and celebrate with me. My aunts and uncle (my dad's sisters and brother) flew in from Arizona and Oregon to celebrate with me. I had not seen them in years, so it was a blessing that they chose to spend a weekend with me. They met Eric......I don't think they were impressed. They were cordial towards him, but didn't really acknowledge him. I was the one that had to keep including him into conversations. Is it because he's white? I mean, my uncle is married to a white woman. This bothered me a bit. This is going to be the guy that I marry. My mom, aunts and uncle are not impressed with him. What will this mean down the road during our marriage? As a gift to myself, I wanted to visit family in Arizona and go to California. Eric had family in California, so this worked out. His uncle (his mom's brother) lived in California, so we made plans to stay with them. We decided that we were going to drive (more Eric than me). Now, I will mention. Eric stopped working at the credit union to focus more on school, so he stayed working part-time at Abercrombie & Fitch. So, for this trip, I was primarily paying for everything, the rental car, gas and any foods we would eat. Thank goodness we were staying with family during this trip. His mom gave him $200.00 to cover him for the week or so we would be out. The side eye emoji needs to go here. Oh, and the rolling eye emoji needs to go here as well. And, maybe the mind blown emoji......

So, we are on the road to California!!! We talked quite a bit during the road trip. Being that we were driving through mountains, Eric did a lot of the driving. We made it to California!!! His uncle and family were really kind to me. Because we weren't married, we couldn't sleep in the same room. Makes sense, that's actually how it should be. Thank goodness his uncle likes to bbq, so that was saving money. We went to the San Diego Zoo (that place is huge), La Jolla Beach, downtown and more. I had a great time!!! Now, it's off to Arizona! We stayed with one of my aunts (thank goodness). I was able to visit my grandma, my grandfather, and my other aunt. Now, at my aunt's place, Eric and I were able to sleep in the same room (I liked how Eric's uncle made us sleep in separate rooms). With us sleeping in the same room, you know sexual temptation was just hanging in the room, **"I say then: Walk in the Spirit, and you shall not fulfill the lust of the flesh. For the flesh lusts against the Spirit, and the Spirit against the flesh; and these are contrary to one another, so that you do not do the things you wish. But if you are led by the Spirit, you are not under the law. Now the works of the flesh are evident, which are adultery, fornication, uncleanness, lewdness, idolatry, sorcery, hatred, contentions, jealousies, outbursts of wrath, selfish ambitions, dissensions, heresies, envy, murders, drunkenness, revelries, and the like; of which I tell you beforehand, just as I also told *you* in the past time, that those who practice such things will not inherit the kingdom of God." – Galatians 5:16-21.** That's the Apostle Paul speaking. I learn more about him later. Yes, the flesh was getting in the way, and there was touching and kissing, but never full intercourse (I've heard horror stories about girls first time. The pain (allergic to), the blood, the soreness.....I didn't want that. We couldn't keep our hands off of each other. Alright, time to head back to Colorado.

I was having issues with my apartment. There was a leak in the roof, and the apartment complex felt as if they didn't need to inform me of the leak. I was talking about it with Eric, and he suggested that I move in with him. This is great!!! We've been talking more and more about getting married and moving, so this will help save money, and we can see what it is like to live together (that's what couples do, right? Move in together before getting married to see what it would be like?). He discussed with his mom, she was excited. I mentioned it to my mom, she was not excited (not surprised). After some thought, I moved in with Eric and his parents (doesn't sound right). Early June 2005, I was out of my apartment. I put all of my furniture in storage, and took myself, my car and clothes over to my 'new' place. This was going to be great!! What could go wrong?

Eric was studying in school to edit movies (I keep praying that I see his name during the credits). He is so talented. He made a few videos, I would be a part of them. He would show off his work, and I would be so proud of him. After a month of me living with him (and his parents), I asked how was he liking it. He said he enjoyed seeing me every day, and liked that we didn't have to drive back and forth to see each other. But, a strain was coming up. He was no longer working at the credit union, but we were still secretive about our relationship. He didn't like the fact that we couldn't be free and walk out in places, holding hands. I completely understood. It had been a habit for so long for us. We only told a few people about our relationship, although, I bet more knew. So, we started to become more open about our relationship. We honestly had nothing to hide. And, who cares who sees us......right?! Deep down, I really didn't want people to see us. Why? Was it because of his age? His skin color? It was like half of Colorado Springs worked at one of the branches for the credit union, but I did understand how he felt. With us being more open about our relationship, Eric had met a young man at school, or did he work with Eric? Either way, I didn't like this young man (we'll call him Trent). I could see a little change in Eric due to the fact that he was hanging out with Trent. Trent had the, 'I don't care' mentality. One night, we went to go hangout at Trent's (why), so that he could help Eric with editing a video. I could tell that Trent had no respect for women. NONE! He would try to talk down to me, or make it seem as if I didn't exist. Why wasn't Eric standing up for me? He would be quiet whenever Trent spoke to me. This wasn't good, and doubts about us began to form.

I wanted a dog!! How do I get one while living in a place that is not really mine? I mentioned it to Eric's mom one day. We talked about how time consuming they could be, and how much work I would have to put in. I was for it. I think I was looking for something to fill a void I was beginning to feel between Eric and me. We weren't talking about marriage much anymore. His mom bought me Wedding planner, and we even went to go look at rings (his mom and I), but Eric seemed to have lost interest. So, a dog can fill this void for now. His mom and I went to a pet store (I know.....I know....). My mind was always set to have a Yorkie. The pet store didn't have one, but they had a Bichon Frise. A what? What do they look like? Ohhhhh................the fluffy white dogs. I don't know..........I really want a Yorkie. Eric's mom was relaying to me (again) about the hard work I will have to put in, as well as the time. I still wasn't sure if I wanted this little fur ball. Eric's mom said this, "If you want her to take you home, you better let her know." Right then, the little fur ball perked up and started licking my chin. I knew I was taking him home. So, I got my little puppy. At two months, he was already a handful. He was very curious and followed me everywhere. I don't know if I got my dog (Kibbles is the name he was given....I know.....I know) to keep Eric close, but it worked for a bit. He would help feed him, take him outside to use the bathroom, his mom would watch Kibbles while I went to work. This was great.

Late October 2005, this is a day I will not forget. Or, should I say, the weekend I will not forget. Once a year, the credit union would partner with an organization where we would help someone paint their house, help in the yard, serve at a soup kitchen, etc.......I volunteered to help paint. So, I spent the day painting with other co-workers. It was fun! We laughed, ate (the homeowner fed us lunch) and painted. Now, I didn't realize that I would be in pain from painting, I mean I was sore. So, once I got 'home', I just wanted to rest, but I knew the fur ball wanted some of my time. Eric came home from school. We said our 'hellos', shared a kiss and talked about our day. As night came, I was getting tired. I was getting ready for bed. Eric came into the bedroom, and I asked him if he could take Kibbles to the bathroom. He made a comment about not being able to do it, or something like that. I was tired and exasperated, so I retorted back, "Can't you help with this? It's not like I am asking for (enter explicit) much." It was under my breath, but you could still hear it. I went upstairs to take the fur ball to the bathroom, and then came back downstairs and went to bed. I later felt him give me a kiss on head.....but, that was it. I woke up in the morning, and he wasn't in bed. He slept out in the family room. My heart dropped. For some reason, I knew this would be the end of our relationship, but didn't want to believe it. I decided to get dressed and go see a movie, to kind of like, clear my head. Eric's mom was willing to watch Kibbles for me. I came back to the house sometime later, and

Eric was gone. He came back late in the day, but he never came downstairs. I sat on the couch and cried. After some much needed tears, I went upstairs to ask his mom if she had any boxes. She did, so I brought them downstairs. I knew I needed to start packing, just didn't have a place to go to (mom moved to Florida). His mom came downstairs sometime later and ask what was going on. I explained to her what happened. She said something like that happened between her and Eric's dad. She left, but came back after they talked, but the time apart was good. I knew this wasn't the case. Eric finally came downstairs, but he didn't speak to me. I started crying again. He went back upstairs to go out. This happened on a Saturday. Sunday morning comes around, and Eric slept in the family room again. I knew this was bad, two nights in a row of not sleeping in bed with me. He was always anxious to sleep with me. My heart dropped again. I believe I spent the day trying to get his attention, love on him, and watch football with him, just to see what he was feeling. Later in the day, I finally asked him what was wrong. I told him that he had not really spoken to me since Friday night. He told me that he didn't want to do this anymore. He felt being pressured into getting married (which we stopped talking about for some time), and that if we did get married, I was going to want to have children quickly because I am older (this is what Trent had told him). He didn't like how I spoke to him and the word I used. He'd been thinking about it for a while. MY HEART DROPPED!!! I cried so hard. I asked if we could work things out, and he didn't want to. After he told me that, he left to go hang out with........Trent! I so was devastated!!! I didn't know what to do. I called a friend and told her what happened. She was livid!! She wanted to come over and fight him. I was still on the phone with her when Eric came back to the house. He kind of looked as if he was regretting his decision, but I wasn't for it. Tomorrow is Monday. How will I function at work? I went to bed crying, and I woke up crying. Kibbles slept with me, while Eric (once again) slept out in the family room. On my way to work, I called one of my closest friends (I will call her Maria). Talk about livid!!! I mean....LIVID!!!! Right away, she told me that once I got off from work, to get my clothes and Kibbles and come stay a few days with her and her family until we figured something out. She told me to not listen to what he had to say, just get my stuff and leave. I called and told my mom, she said she didn't like him anyway, and told me not to move in

16

with him (not something I needed to hear right at the moment). I got to work, and I am sure I was a mess. Another good friend was working, so I asked if she could come outside. I told her what happened, and she was livid!!! She gave me hugs and asked if there was anything she could do. I told her to just pray for me (I'm reaching out to God now, because I was barely doing it during this relationship). Everyone at work could tell I was off. People wanted to beat up Eric for me. There were upset that someone hurt me. I did do what Maria said, I went to the house to get my clothes and Kibbles. Eric tried talking with me, but I told him I had to leave (he was saying that I could still live there with him......WHAT?!?! (Please enter wide eyed emoji here.....like 5 times). I packed, and went to Maria's. She was upset still. I was hurting, and she didn't like seeing her friend hurting. She said I could stay with them until I knew what I wanted to do. I wanted to die, really. A relationship that I gave two years of myself to, was over. I think I wrote all of my heartache in a journal (I do still have that journal). I prayed for Eric and me to get back together, but did I really want us back together?

The few days, actually turned into 5 months. Like, I helped Maria and her family move into their new home. I actually had my own room and bathroom, it was like it wasn't a thing. Eric tried to connect at times, I had to stop responding to him, but he was all I knew for over two years. His mom wanted to meet up for lunch one day, and we did. We talked, but I told her this would be the last time we see each other. I didn't think it was fair or right for us to communicate when her son and I were no longer together. Oh, before I forget. Around December of 2005, I decided to get all of my stuff from Eric's parents place and put into storage. This way, I didn't have to come back and forth, or find excuses to 'visit'. I had to do that in November of 2005 because I had my wisdom teeth pulled (an appointment I made before the breakup). His mom had already planned to watch over me and help me heal, so she did that. Eric was gone that week (thank goodness). I had friends come and visit, so that was helpful and soothing. So, back to the getting all of my stuff. Me and a few friends (they were kind enough to help) went to the house to start packing the remainder of my stuff. His mom opened the door, and looked so sad. I told her it would be okay. We went downstairs to start packing. We were on a mission!!! Guess what?! Eric was on the couch!!! He didn't bother to help with the packing. He said he wasn't feeling well. FOR REAL?! Thank you for showing me your true colors. As my friends and I were packing, I was in the bathroom getting my lotions, and bath cleansers together (Victoria's Secret was getting all of my money), when his mom came in. She was so heartbroken. She was crying!!! I was surprised that I was not crying. She told me how sorry she was, and was hoping we would get back together. I told her it wasn't meant to be and that God has someone wonderful for Eric, and that she would love her more than she loved me (what was happening? I am mentioning God again?). We hugged, and it was time to roll out. Eric finally got off the couch and walked upstairs to walk me out, but I told him to not bother since he didn't feel well. I hugged his mom again, and that was the last time I saw Eric and his mom.

Welcome 2006!!!! A new year, a new beginning. I was done with school, my mom and sister left Colorado, and I was no longer in a relationship. So, what do I do? I prepared to move.....leave the Rockies (I never did like driving in snow). So, where am I going to move to? Well, my friends did not want me moving at all. I felt like I was overstaying at Maria's (they have a new house). It was time for me to go. Where am I going to move to? Hmmm........how about........hmmmmm..........I've always wanted to live in Florida. The beach, the warmth, the beach, the beach, and different cultures, and the beach. Florida it is. Once my decision was made, I began to prepare for being with my mom and sister again (Lord, please help), the heat (humidity is good for the skin and hair), and whatever was in store for me and my fur ball. I knew I wouldn't live in Colorado forever, I just didn't see me leaving like this. I am so thankful for Maria and her family. The fact that they didn't just kick me out.......that is friendship. Such amazing hearts. During the toughest time of my life, Maria and her family were there for me. I do thank God for them every day. So, it's time to leave my old life, a relationship I thought would go on forever, a heart that was broken, and start anew. It's time to get back on the road again (do you hear the song?). On my way Florida......

REFLECTION

"Lean on, trust in, and be confident in the LORD with all of your heart and mind and do not rely on your own insight or understanding. In all your ways know, recognize, and acknowledge Him, and He will direct and make straight and plain your paths." – Proverbs 3:5-6 AMPC

Breakups are hard, whether when dating or friendship. Can you think of a time when a relationship that was so important to you, fell apart? How did you feel? Hurt? Angry? Betrayed? Who did you turn to? Was it God? A friend? A family member? A co-worker? It can be easier said than done (I really do not like that saying), but turning to God is the best thing anyone of us can do. Trusting in Him and His ways will keep you on the straight path. Do you trust Him to lead you on the path He has for you? Write out your thoughts about that relationship that hurt you. Was God in it? Would it have been different if He had been?

CHAPTER 2
WELCOME TO FLORIDA:
The Meeting

"Lean on, trust in, and be confident in the LORD with all of your heart and mind and do not rely on your own insight or understanding. In all your ways know, recognize, and acknowledge Him, and He will direct and make straight and plain your paths."

– Proverbs 3:5-6 AMPC

Leaving a broken heart in Colorado Springs, Colorado, I head down to Orlando, Florida. I will be honest, I've always wanted to live in Florida (remember.....beach, culture, beach, warm weather, beach, beach and beach), so I figured this was the place I was supposed to move to. I was attending church while living in Colorado. Actually, I was attending more frequently than when I was living in Baton Rouge, LA. But, that doesn't mean I was growing closer to God. I lifted up a prayer before, during and after my drive from Colorado to Florida, I knew I was being watched over. God does that, you know. Even when we turn our backs to Him, or don't even have a serious relationship with Him, He still watches over us. The drive was smooth. Left Colorado in the wee hours of the morning, on March 17, 2006 (my mom always tells me I am good with dates). Me and my little fur ball, on the road. We made it to Dallas, Texas that same day (Texas is the biggest and longest state to drive through). Got a hotel for the night, and thank goodness Kibbles was quiet. We checked out early the next morning, and headed towards Baton Rouge, LA so that I could spend a few days with my grandma. I hadn't seen her since I left in 2000 to move back to Colorado. Made it to my grandma's later that Saturday evening. I am early bird, so for me, it is important to get out on the road before traffic starts up. I covered good ground. While in Baton Rouge, I visited my old job, Tony's Seafood. If you ever go to Baton Rouge, be sure to visit this place. It's a family owned business and the food is really good. I also visited family and some friends. It was good spending time with grandma. She was able to meet Kibbles (she called him 'Pebbles'). After about four or five days with grandma, it was time to head to Florida. After about a week, from the time I left Colorado, I made it to Florida. It was time I really needed, time to reflect about what my next steps would be, **"A man's heart plans his way, But the LORD directs his steps." - Proverbs 16:9 NKJV**. This will be a good move for me, maybe......I'll meet my husband here in a few years.

I am in Florida, and I am ready to look for a job. Mom says to take some time to rest and relax, but I need to work. I still have bills to pay. I did have money in my account, plus a couple of more checks coming to me from the credit union, so I wasn't hurting, but I wanted to work. I thought that I would for sure get a job at a bank or credit union being that I used to work for a financial institution. I mean, I was a loan officer by the time I left the credit union, so you would think, "She'd make a great employee." This was not the case. The first week or two of being in Florida, I did take time to relax, but I am so used to being busy that I really needed to get out. So, I began job hunting. I was applying at credit unions, banks, Walgreen's, Lockheed Martin, you know, big places to work at. I mean, I didn't want to toot my own horn, but I was a catch for a good employee. Why wasn't anyone hiring me? I wasn't getting it. "Why is this happening to me, LORD? Why can't I find a job?" I was starting to worry. Would I ever work? Well, I saw somewhere (a commercial, a billboard, newspaper.......) that a national rental car company was hiring. Hmmmm.....maybe I will give it try. Now, let me fill you in about the travel arrangements. My mom lived (lives) way out from Orlando. Like, over an hour (in Colorado Springs, everything was close). So, I am driving all over the place looking for a job, which is using up gas, which costs money.........a job is needed. I head over across town to fill out an application. Again, I get a spot on interview (my mom trained us well). I am told that I will receive a phone call to setup an interview. Alright! Come on, Lord! Within the next day or two, I receive a phone call to setup my interview. The interview is set, and I go on to wow them!! Again, not to toot my own horn, but I can strike up conversations to the point where it seems like we've known each other for years. And, that's what I did with the interviewer. We were in there for almost two hours. She literally told me that she forgot she was interviewing me (nailed it!). I received an offer within a day, and was to start my new job within a week. Okay, so adding something new on my resume......working for a national rental car company. I've rented cars before, but to work on the other side will be very different.

As you know, most jobs, if not all, require training. I don't mind training, but I am a more of a visual learner, so sitting in a room for 8-9 hours will put me to sleep (note for future training classes). It needs to be interactive and interesting. If you are speaking directly from the slides......................just insert sleeping emoji here. With that said, the training was about two weeks!!! That's a long time to just sit there, and not do a whole lot. For me, two weeks is a lot. I will admit, there was a lot to learn about renting out a car; did the customer want an Economy size car (remember the Chevy Aveo.....looked like an Easter egg?), or a Full size car (Chevy Impala)? How long would they have the rental? Was the rental staying in state (you'd be surprise how many people would say 'yes', but then the car would end up in New York??)? Would they be the only driver (again......you'd be surprised)? Would the rental be on debit/credit (you could pay cash once the car was returned)? And, the eternal question......................would the customer be using the company's insurance, or their own? They trained us a lot on that one. Don't stop selling until you get three 'no's'. That's a lot of no's, and that's a lot of pushing. I wasn't a fan of that part. I am a good seller (my retail days), but I wasn't pushy. I wouldn't want that forced on me. It was pretty much, get the sale however you can. Ummmm.......I will stick with not being pushy, and be honest. Basically, if you are in a rental for a weekend, it's not bad to get the Basic Coverage (back then, it was around $14.00/day. Not sure if it's gone up since 2006). If you were in it longer, then I would mention it once, and not bring it up again. If a customer had American Express, the Black Card, you could forget about it.

Within the national rental car company, they wanted each of us to eventually have our own branch, it was like having our own business. You start out 6 months of being a Management Trainee (MT), then three months being a Management Assistant (MA). During the MA period, one would study to become an Assistant Manager. After three months of being a MA, it would be time to take your test to become an Assistant Manager. The test was really an Area Manager, two Branch Managers and your Assistant Manager (for moral support) asking you questions about your job. Like, how would you handle a situation if a car was not returned when promised. Or, if two employees are not getting along (because that never happens). Or, if a car was stolen (trust me, it has happened), or if the insurance company has stopped paying on the rental, and the customer is to take over, but you're not getting in touch with customer. You know, the typical stuff. You answer the questions correctly and confidently (and you would know by the way your Assistant Manager and Area Manager would give nods or smiles), that you pretty much passed and was on your way to becoming an Assistant Manager. If you were on track, that would all happen within 9-12 months. Then, of course, you can move up to be a Branch Manager, Area Manager, District Manager, and so on. I was not sure if I wanted all of that, but I did want to move up as much as I could.

Let me tell you, there are so many stories I have about working at a national rental car company. I started out working in a branch that was kind of near my mom's, but not really (it was like 45 minutes away). The hours were long, like...................long. 0730 am to 600 pm, and really, you had to be to work around 0700 am and wouldn't leave until 630 pm. That was Monday-Friday. On Saturdays, it was 0900 am – 200 pm. The only day I had off was Sunday (I didn't like that). Working six days a week, working over 10 hour days out of the five days, washing cars in the Florida heat......in panty hose, with customers yelling at you or calling you to pick them up (women went by themselves to pick up customers. That wasn't safe at all.), standing outside with the customers, in the Florida heat, to go over their contract. I wasn't expecting this. I don't remember them mentioning any of this during the training (or, was I sleeping when they did?). I wasn't enjoying the long hours and being in the heat (who wears pantyhose in Florida?), but I met some really cool people.

I can be an extrovert, I mean, I do like being around people, and the traveling to different locations while growing up, really helped me to be able to communicate with others. I am so thankful for that upbringing. So, it took me no time to in getting to know my co-workers, and going to the clubs. I like to dance, so going to the clubs was a thing for quite a few years. I never went looking for a man. I knew my husband was not at the club like that. And, I didn't like guys dancing all over me, no, I am fine by myself. The first branch I worked at, it was a given that every Friday night we were going out after work. This meant, I had to hurry and drive 45 minutes to an hour to get home, take a shower, change clothes, and assume my mom would watch my dog and then head all the way to Downtown Disney. The club scene used to be called, 'Pleasure Island' back then. It would be about 20 of us deep in the clubs, to laugh, dance, eat and, for others, drink. I was never much of a drinker, plus I always wanted to be careful about what was in my drink. Well, the first night I hung out with my Assistant

Manager and the rest of my branch, he had a drink. A co-worker and I were curious, so we asked what he was drinking. Instead of telling us, he bought us each the drink. I kept saying no, but then I took it. Why did I do that?! As I was taking the shot, I could literally feel it go through my body, almost like.......it was a drug (which I had never done before). Come to find out, the drink was called, 'Liquid Cocaine.' WHAT?!?! Why would one drink that?! Well, silly me, I did because I didn't ask the right questions, and I should've walked away. Girl, can I tell you, that drink messed me up for the rest of the night. My co-worker and I were both dizzy, that we could barely stand. I had another co-worker who got kicked out of Pleasure Island!! Who gets kicked out of Disney club area?! Exactly, what are you doing to get to that point? He said he was banned. Really?! You're banned?! Too bad because I thought he was kind of cute, but he was too young for me...........and.............he got banned from a Disney club. He definitely was not for me. So, as the night wound down, we were all preparing to go home. My head was still spinning from the drink I had some 5 hours earlier, so I figured that I would take a quick nap in the car. I didn't want my mom knowing that I was out so late and had a drink that was doing me in. Yes, I know I was 29 going on 30, but still had to respect my mom's home. Remember that quick nap? How about I woke up around 400 am!!! WHAT?!?! 3 hours sleeping in the car?! In the parking lot?! And no one was concerned, like, not even the security guard?! Was the security guard even still there??? So, I hurried and got home (still drove the speed limit). I don't know if my mom was awake or asleep when I got home a little before 500 am, but I do know that mothers do not fully sleep when their child (ren) are out in the streets. Guess what?! I had to work that Saturday. Yay me!!! I slept for another hour, and then got up and got ready for work. It was like I was living a life that I didn't live back during my high school days. I got to work, on time, and let me tell you, that was a rough day! Half of us that went out that Friday night, had to work that Saturday. And, we were not doing well. I didn't pressure any customer to take the damage waiver. I tried to sit down as much as I could, and I stayed inside as much as possible (it can get pretty hot in Florida in April). After work, we all went to Chili's to eat, and man was I hungry. But, that food helped soak up that drink that was still pulsing throughout my body. That was last time I had that drink. I knew I had to cut back on hanging out with these people for my well- being. Especially, if there was going to be a lot of drinking and being out until the wee hours of the morning. I used to go out back in my college days, but not like this. For the next three months, I hung out on the weekends with my co-workers. Friday nights were our nights. After three months, it was time to rotate to another branch.

So, now I am working at a branch in a dealership. I didn't like working at the dealership. The customers never took the damage waiver and they all had attitude. Of course, my attitude was coming back. People were not going to talk to me anyway they wanted to. I had to be careful though, some complaints were coming in and that could look bad if I wanted to move up. Working at the dealership was helping me getting used to another demographic of customers. We had to know how to handle all types of customers. I kind of bumped heads with the Assistant Manager. I can be headstrong, so I found myself being rebellious......is that the word? I was becoming miserable. To work all day in an environment where I was not being respected (was it because I am a woman, or African American or both?). I would cry out to God, "Why is this happening?" Mind you, I did thank God for helping me get the job with the national rental car company, I just wasn't seeking Him like I needed to.....like I should've been. But, I wanted Him to take me out of this situation. Do you ever pray those type of prayers? "Lord, please help me. Get me out of this situation. I promise I'll do better." God knows the truth, He knows us. He created us. Sometimes we ask God to take us out of a situation, when He is actually using it to strengthen us and drawing us closer to Him. **"Even when I walk through the darkest valley, I will not be afraid, for *You* are close beside me. Your rod and your staff protect and comfort me." – Psalm 23:4 NLT emphasized.** Being that I wasn't attending church during this time (yes, I fell off, again), I didn't know what God was doing. I knew I was lifting up prayers, but they were empty prayers. Have you ever lifted up empty prayers to God? No? Just me? I am being completely honest. Empty prayers, or known as 'vain' prayers, are useless prayers. **Matthew 6:7 reads, "When you pray, don't babble on and on as the Gentiles do. They think their prayers are answered merely by repeating their words again and again."** This is how I was feeling, just lifting up prayers to a God I wasn't sure was real. I mean, if He was, I would be in Colorado, or Illinois, married to the guy who didn't want to be with me (none of that makes sense, right?!). That was how I felt. So, you can say that I was angry at God, but didn't really realize it at the time. And, I believe I was taking the anger I had towards God, out on my Assistant Manager and the customers. There was still some hurt from the breakup. I mean, it hadn't been a year, so the pain was still there. Eric was my first boyfriend, and I thought that we would be together forever (I sound like one of those romance novels). Life is hard.

So, now it's time for my rotation to work at the airport location. We were required to work at the airport for three months during our internship. Now, I had to get used to working at the airport because the hours were different. It wasn't Monday-Saturday anymore (thank You, Lord), no, now I am working 5 days a week, but various days. For example (I hope this doesn't confuse you); I could work from 10-7 on Monday and Tuesday, work 11-8 on Wednesday, off Thursday and Friday, and work 2-10 on Saturday and 12-7 on Sunday. Then it would be different the next week. With this type schedule, guess what happened......back on the club scene!!!! Yes, I was with a group that enjoyed going out (and so do I), so this worked out great! So, the example schedule I gave you meant this.................going out to dinner after work on Wednesday, discuss which club we are going to Thursday night and time. Rest up all day Thursday to go out later that night, then discuss which club we are going to Friday night. Rest up all day Friday to go out Friday night. And, then meet up for lunch on Saturday before going to work. I enjoyed this. I liked being back out and hanging around a new group of people. Again, I was not out looking for a man. I will say, the going out was putting a strain between my mom and I. Really, a strain that was already there, but it deepened. I was just coming in and out of her home, barely spending time with my little fur ball and I had attitude. I was disrespecting my mom, but I didn't know why. Did it have something to do with how she would say, 'You're just like your dad.' And, she would say this often. Being that my parents got a divorced when I was 4, I wonder if she was still harboring ill feelings towards my dad. And, being that I favor him (looks wise), was that bothering her? Was I a hurting reminder of what transpired between my mom and dad all those years ago? At the time, I didn't care. I was going out.

Now, working at the airport location was no piece of cake. The going out helped us unwind from the yelling customers (why are you guys way out here? It says that you (the rental company) is located at the airport (on the confirmation it also reads that a shuttle would you bring to the airport)). Standing out in the hot weather to have the customer sign the contract. Looking for vehicles that were dropped off at the airport, but..........nowhere to be found (where is that Ford Focus?). Walking to the very back of the lot.....and, I mean the back, to get a car for a customer who didn't want the vehicle that was located right up front. Oh, and did I mention that it had rain the night prior, so the car the customer wants is stuck in the mud?! Yes, that happened quite a bit. Or, dealing with a customer returning a car, but....has.....bullet holes in it. Can someone please explain why the Ford Taurus has bullet holes in the car? And, why are the holes covered up with duct tape? The tape doesn't match the color of the car. Or, a customer refusing to take the damage waiver, crashes the car before leaving the lot, pays the deductible, gets another rental, and still refuses the damage waiver. I am telling you I cannot make these stories up. So, going out and unwinding seemed almost justifiable. I needed to unwind and really try to forget about my ex-boyfriend (probably the first time I've said that, ex-boyfriend. A pride thing). Again, I was not looking for a man, and there were no sexual activities going on. Going out and having a few drinks helped me to forget about Eric, or so I thought.

After my time at the airport, it was time to head back to the branches. Actually, it was time for me to study and prepare to become a Management Assistant. The Assistant Manager I hung out with while working at the airport, started helping me study back then. So, once I got back to the branches, I was put at a location that would be slow, still help me with my numbers and give me time to study. The branch they put me to work was located in a hotel. It was a nice hotel, kind of a fancy one. You know, the type where the rooms are like $300/night, your name is on the t.v. and phone, valet parking and bellboys to take your luggage to your room for you. The traffic for rental cars was slow, but when someone did come over to rent a car, I was going to upsell them. Upsell means, if a customer/guest had a reservation for a Full size car at $49.99/day, I could try to rent to the customer/guest a Premium size car for $54.99/day. Now, if a customer/guest did not have reservation, well, here we go (insert smiley face emoji here). If a customer/guest needed a Full size car, and the system read $49.99/day, I would rent it for $59.99/day due to the fact that they did not have a reservation. And, being that I was the only rental car company on sight, it was pretty easy to rent out cars. I've rented out SUVs for about $103.99/day. And, the guest would take the damage waiver. Yeah, the traffic was slow, but the three to five customers/guests I would help, made up for the reason why there was a branch, 'satellite branch' in the hotel. And...I...was...working...it!! Making money for the branch, studying to be a Management Assistant and.......am I being checked out?

Next to my little desk, was a young lady who worked selling discounted tickets to the amusement parks and other attractions. *Natalie and I became friends pretty quickly. She told me that one of the bellhops was interested in me. ME?!?! REALLY?!?! Who is he? Right when I asked her, he walked by. Okay, he's cute. Natalie told me that he asked about me. Oh, really?!? Ladies, you know what that means......need to step up my game a bit; wear a cute dress....a cute fitting dress, make sure my hair is on point, and of course, walk by a few times so that he can see me (a girl has to go to the bathroom.....even if it is way on the other side). Natalie was encouraging me to speak with him, like say 'Hi.' Okay, so actually speak, like say something when I walk by to go to the bathroom (note: there was a bathroom right near me)? Ready for this, Danielle? Ready to meet this guy for the first time? Ready to dive into a relationship? Ready for this new adventure? Okay.....let's go!!

The next day, I decided to walk over to the counter where the bellboys (or, is it bellhops) were standing, and say 'Hello" to the guy that kept checking me out (I was low-key checking him out as well). It was like he was waiting for me because when I walked up, he came around from the counter to say, "Hi" to me. We told each other our names, and the conversation went like this:

Me: "My name is Danielle."
Him: "My name is *Jason."
Me: "How are you?"
Jason: "I'm good. How are you?"

Me: "I am well. I see you've been checking me out (straight to the point)."

Jason: "I have, but you've been checking me out too."

Me: "True. Are you working all day?"

Jason: "Yes, I just started my shift." (By this time, his boss comes out, but his boss liked me).

Me: "I'll let you get back to work. Don't work too hard. Talk to you later."

My heart wasn't racing at all (will my heart ever race for a man?). I wasn't nervous. It was normal for me to go and speak to someone, remember my upbringing. I wasn't sure what would take place, but by the end of the day.....I had Jason's number. On my way home from work, I started contemplating what took place on this day. It was a small conversation, but it was enough to where Jason gave me his number. It was enough to show Jason that I was interested in him, and that his interest in me heightened. Should I be giddy? Is this something to tell my friends back in Colorado about? Was that meeting going to lead to more? Let's see, shall we.

REFLECTION

"But seek first the kingdom of God and His righteousness, and all these things shall be added to you." - Matthew 6:33 NKJV

As you read in Chapter 2, I left Colorado because of pain. If I stayed, I would see my ex- boyfriend, or hear of him being with someone else. Too much for my eyes, ears.....heart. I figured it was best for me to leave. Did you hear/read what I said? I.......I thought it was best for me to leave. I allowed my heart and emotions to get in the way. The prophet Jeremiah tells us about the heart in Chapter 17 verse 9, **"The heart is deceitful above all things, and it is exceedingly perverse and corrupt *and* severely, mortally sick! Who can know it [perceive, understand, be acquainted with his *(her)* own heart and mind]? [Matthew 13:15-17; Mark 7:21-23 and Ephesians 4:20-24]. Emphasis added AMPC.** The heart is deceitful!!! We can't trust our hearts. We can't trust our feelings. I look back, and if I had allowed God full access to my life, I don't think I would've left Colorado. Like **Matthew 6:33** states, seek first the Kingdom of God........meditate on that......*seek first the Kingdom of God.....SEEK GOD!!!* I didn't seek God, I wasn't trying to seek God. I allowed my heartbreak to rule everything, including my heart. Because I serve a God that is so loving, forgiving, and merciful and full of grace, He didn't punish me (people think that God is just full of wrath and waiting for us to mess up). He wasn't disappointed in me. I'm learning that He can take our mess, and turn them into messages. What mess has God turned into a message for you? Take a moment to reflect, and write it down.

Prayer: Heavenly Father, thank You so much for Your gracious love, mercy, grace (Your unmerited favor) and forgiveness. I deserve none of those, but You found me worthy to receive all of them. Thank You for turning my mess into a message. Thank You for turning a stubborn heart into a malleable one for You. Thank You for calling me Your own. In Jesus' Name. Amen.

CHAPTER 3
SILENT TEARS:
What Happened?

"Hear my prayers, O Lord! Listen to my cries for help! Don't ignore my tears…"

Psalm 39:12 NLT

I began working at the satellite branch at the hotel around late November/early December 2006. Around that time is when I met Jason. We played the flirting game during this time, you know, the looking at each other while walking by, or the, little hand waves, or the winks at each other (more him than me), little small talks, those games. Do people still play those games anymore? I know times are changing, and people want to get straight to the point, so I was just wondering. Around January 2007, Jason finally asked if I wanted to go out. Now, I had his number, and I gave him mine, but we did not really call each or text each other during that time. It wasn't until he asked me out that we actually started texting each other. And, that was more for setting up our date. I am sure he told his coworkers about our upcoming date, because they would kind of look at me. What were the looks for? Should I be concerned? Why the smirks? Am I just being paranoid?

Early February 2007 was the first date for Jason and me. How old is Jason? Should I ask? Our first date was one that I promised I would not do again. Not for a first date. We went to see a movie (forgot the name). Going to see a movie for a first, second or third date, is not good. You can't talk to each other, and get to know one another. I am the type, if you talk during a movie, I am upset. I paid to see the people on the screen, not the conversations around me. Thank goodness Jason understood this. As were waiting in line to purchase our tickets, we met at a theater that was kind of in the middle for the both of us (still far from my mom's), we were able to have our small talk. I asked him his age (he was 23). What is the deal with me and younger guys? Do I look that young? I am not interested in being a 'cougar.' I was beginning to feel a complex. Should I tell him my age? He may not want to see me if I do. He asked me mine, '30' (with so much hesitation). He said it wasn't a big deal. He was surprised because he said I didn't look like it. Whew! If he was good with it, then I was good with it. Still wasn't sure why younger men were attracted to me. After the movie, we walked out to our cars (he did walk me to my car). He said he had a good time (why did this make me feel weary). He wanted a kiss, but I told him it was our first date, and that I didn't kiss on the first date (plus, I had not dated a lot of guys, so I was afraid that I wouldn't be a good kisser). He accepted it (or, did he?). We told each other goodnight and to get home carefully. I would say that the date was a success. I was more nervous about him finding out my age, than him trying to get a kiss. We'll see if there will be another date.

I didn't work at the hotel the next day, but Jason did text me. He said he had good time the other night, and that he wondered if I would go on another date with him. Of course! I had a good time as well. This next date would be dinner (good, we will be able to talk some). We met at a restaurant near him (remember where I lived at the time). I think we ate at Red Lobster. Remember how that used to be the place to go for a date? We talked and got to know each other a bit more, I mean, enough to know each other within a few hours. After dinner, he invited me to his place. I told him no and that I had to get back and get ready for work. He wanted a kiss, but I told him no. He said it wasn't the first date, and I agreed to that, but still was not ready to kiss him. He seemed fine with that, at least that's what it looked like. We wished each other a goodnight, and he told me to text him when I got home. The second date seemed to have gone well.

We started talking on the phone by this point. Now, being that mom lived way out from Orlando, the connection at times wouldn't work too well. We would basically talk during the night, so I had to literally be in a certain spot in my bedroom to talk on the phone. There would be times that I would be lying in bed with an arm up just to get better connection. Who looked ridiculous? And, whose conversation would be short due to that? Me and mine. Plus, Jason would call around 10 pm, and I had to get up around 4 am to get ready for work. This was not going to work. We'll have to find a better time to talk on the phone. But, this was the beginning stage, and I was just excited that a guy was interested in me. Very sad, but true.

Jason wanted me to meet his friends, so he wanted me to come over to his place. I was weary and asked if we could meet like at the Ale House (it's a Florida staple). I wanted to be in an area that was more open and with people around. So, I met a few of his close friends, which included his roommate. They seemed nice, friendly and they liked me. That's a plus, right? So, I hung out for a few hours with Jason and his friends. Afterwards, he tried to get me to go back to his place. I still said no, and still no kiss. I wasn't trying to play the 'hard to get' game, I just wasn't ready to be completely alone with Jason. Should that be a RED flag? I was more comfortable with meeting and hanging out with him in public areas.

Well, Jason was having a bbq at his place, and wanted me to come over. Now, being where I lived, if you wanted me to hangout, you had to tell me well in advance. It truly was a hassle, and an inconvenience, to get ready and drive out about an hour or so to hangout and then drive back home. But, Jason had called early enough, and I was ready just in case I was going to see a movie, So, I went over to his place to hangout for a while. His friends were there, and a few other ladies. We laughed, ate and I listened to them tell stories (man, they are young). As the day went on, people started leaving. I called my mom to let her know that I was still out and would be home shortly. The day turned into evening, and it was just me, Jason and his roommate. His roommate left to go hangout with a friend, so it was just Jason and me. We talked some, and then I was feeling an urge to leave. What's this feeling about? Why do I feel uneasy? I told Jason that I needed to go, and he asked if he could kiss me. It had been about a month since we've been seeing each other. And, did he officially ask me to be his girlfriend? I don't remember him asking me. I remember it vividly. He was sitting on the edge of the couch, and he was pulling me towards him (oh goodness! Will he think I'm a bad kisser?), and we started kissing. I will be honest, my leg didn't kick up (isn't that how it's supposed to go, and which leg is it?), but it was nice to be kissed. He, on the other hand, was left breathless. Not sure if it was an act (now that I think about it), but he enjoyed the kiss. He wanted more, and I told him no. He kept trying to be persistent, but I stood firm and finally went home.

Jason and I were entering our two months of dating, so I was starting to hang out at his place quite a bit. His friends would tease him saying that he didn't deserve me and, that I was too good for him. I told a few friends in Colorado about Jason. A few co-workers knew about him, but I didn't go into detail. He would tell me that I was 'too' perfect for him, and wonder what I saw in him. I think I gave him the typical answer, 'You're cute, funny and I like being around you." Not really an in depth answer, right? I should've spoke of his qualities and future, but I didn't. Did I not see them? Was I settling just to be with someone? Was I afraid that he would breakup with me? When I asked him the same question, his answer was very different, "You're beautiful, with a great upbringing. You have so much potential. I learn from you, and I enjoy being around you. I am not sure I can offer anything to you because you are so good." A little more different from my answer. Now, he wasn't really the 'bad boy' type like he thought he was. He was shorter than me (I prefer a man taller than me), and our conversations were.....just......not.......that entertaining. But, he likes me and I am doing more than just staying at home on the weekends. I can endure this.

I found myself staying out late on Saturdays and Sundays (thank goodness the branch is closed on Sundays). It seemed to be the only time Jason and I could hangout. Getting home late on those Sundays were killers at times. I had to get up around 4 am to get ready for work, which meant, I could not be going to bed late. Then, for Jason to call and want to talk on the phone for a bit. So, we started adding Friday nights to our hangouts. Probably wasn't a good idea being that I had to work on Saturdays as well, but I wanted to see him.

Late April 2007, I was hanging out with Jason at his apartment. It had to be on a Saturday or Sunday because I can see that it was mid-afternoon. It was a Sunday. We were hanging out and talking. Then one of his friends came over. He was going through an issue, so Jason spoke with him for a bit to see if he could help out. I was ready to go home, but Jason wanted me to hangout a little longer. The three of us agreed that we were hungry, and tried to think of a place to go and eat. Hooters was the place of choice (not my choice). Jason and I rode together, and his friend followed behind. We hung out at Hooters for a bit, just talking and allowing Jason's friend to let out more steam. I really wish Jason hung out with more males that had dreams of working to own their own business, or working up the ladder at their current jobs.......seeking their potential. Listening to Jason's friend made me think of all this. It's getting dark, so I better get going. Jason and I head back to his place so that I can get my car, but he wants me to hangout for a bit longer. I told him that I really can't stay long because I have to work the next day, and I've been out all day. I call my mom to let her know that I was hanging out with friends, and that I would be home soon.

Jason and I are on the couch watching t.v. and talking. Then, he begins to try to kiss me. Weeks prior, he would try to get me to have sex with him. I told him no. We just started dating (are we official?), and I wasn't ready for that yet. He would use the line, "I want to be closer to you and having sex with you will make me feel closer." Now, I never heard that before, but I wasn't falling for that. He was going to have to wait. Now, we are on the couch kissing and touching, but I pushed him away and said no touching. He would go back to kissing me, and try touching me again. By this time, I told him that I was leaving. I got up from the couch to head out. He was apologizing and telling me that he wouldn't touch me anymore. I believed him, I really believed him. Again, I was trying to leave, but we started kissing (again). Next thing I know, we are in his bedroom. How did we get here? Did I walk in here with him? Did he walk me into the bedroom? The kissing kept going......why didn't I stop the kissing? Next thing, we are on the bed, and I am on my back, he's on top of me. I push him off of me, and tell him that I didn't want to have sex with him. I wanted to leave. He told me that he just wanted to kiss me.....I gave into that. I gave into him wanting to kiss me. I was on my back again, and my shorts were down.....as well as my underwear. When did this happen? He pulled down his pants and underwear....and.....I froze. I couldn't move. Why can't I move? Why can't I scream? He was still on top of me, and he was reaching for his dresser drawer.....for a condom. Why am I just laying here? Why can't I move? If I push him off, will he attack me? Will there be a fight? Will he hit me? I just laid there as he put the condom on. I just laid there as he entered into me......I just laid there as he raped me. I just laid there and listened to his heavy breathing....I just laid there. I had an 'outer body' experience. It was like, I left my body while the rape was taking place. After a few minutes.......it was over. He got off of me and started to pull up his underwear and shorts. It took me a moment to move, but as soon as I could.....I moved.....slow. It seemed like everything was moving slow, me sitting up, pulling up my underwear and shorts, and me getting out of bed. I had no feeling in my body, it was if I didn't return to my body, if that makes sense. Like, I was still lingering, not wanting to get back into my body. It was as if.......my mind and senses knew what took place, but my body didn't. After a few more minutes had passed by, I was finally able to move.....in a faster pace. Mind and senses were connecting with my body again. I have to hurry and get out of here. I need to leave. I NEED TO LEAVE!!! COME ON, DANIELLE!!!! MOVE FASTER!!!! But, I wasn't moving faster, I mean, I was moving, just not at light speed. I finally get to the front door, and he's right next to me.........why is he next to me? Why won't the door open? Help me get out of here! I get outside and walk to my car, with my head down. He was talking to me, but I couldn't 'hear' him. I need to leave....NOW!!!! Why is the walk to my car so long?! I finally get to my car, and get in. He tells me that "he had a great time." A great time? Was he there? I could feel tears coming to my eyes, and I didn't want him to see my tears. I think he said to call him when I got home, but I went 'deaf' again, so I didn't respond.

I couldn't leave from his place fast enough. Before I left out of the parking lot, I started crying. The drive back to my mom's would take about an hour. What just happened? Was I raped? No, I wasn't raped because I didn't scream, and there was no fighting......no struggle. So, I wasn't raped.....right? Wait........did I agree to have sex? No......I remember saying no. How did I get into the bedroom? Did I yell at all? Why did I just lay there? Why didn't I fight? Why me? What did I do to deserve this? I can't breathe......I can't breathe.....I CAN'T BREATHE!!!! When I get home, what will I tell my mom? Do I tell her? Do I tell my sister? Please let them be asleep when I get home. No questions.....please. PLEASE!!! No tears, no tears, no tears. If they are awake, no tears. Please, no tears!! Oh, I am home. How did I get home? I drove, right?! Get it together....get it together.....get it.......why am I crying??? Get it together. Gather yourself, get out of the car, and get into the house. Go straight to your room. Please, God, if you are there, please let me just make it to my room with no questions. Okay, yes, I am in my room. I need to take a shower. I feel so......dirty. Am I sore? Why am I sore? My body feels tense. What happened? I can't tell anyone. What will people think of me? What do I think of me? He took my virginity. Where's the proof?

REFLECTION

"The thief comes only in order to steal and kill and destroy..." John 10:10a AMPC

Has anything ever been taken from you? ANYTHING???? How did you feel? Was it something you cherished? How did you feel? What emotions were going through you? Anger? Hurt? Betrayal? Lost? Sad? Sickened? Write it out below.

CHAPTER 4
STATISTICS: Am I One?

"For a righteous man falls seven times and rises again, but the wicked are overthrown by calamity. [Job 5:19; Psalm 34:19; 37:24; Micah 7:8]"

Proverbs 24:16, AMPC

The questions began to overwhelm me.....you know.....the ones running around in my head. The questions I asked myself over and over again.

"Why did this happen?" "Why did this happen to *me*?" "Why didn't I fight back?" "Was it my fault?" "Will I be judged (this was a new question that entered my mind)?" "How will my mom look at me.....if I told her?" "Did it really happen?" "Was I really raped?" "God, why did you (notice the lowercase of 'y') let him rape me?" "Why didn't you stop him?" "Was it because I wasn't saved (another new question)?" "Would this have happened if I were saved?" "Who do I tell?" "Do I tell anyone?" "Will anyone believe me?"

We know that sexual violence is prevalent in today's society. Actually, it is encouraged (movies, television, books, songs, etc.......). Why? Because we live in a fallen world, and we listen to the lies more than the truth. During my research (trust me, I didn't want to do this), I found so much information. Here are some numbers:

- As of 1998, 17.7 million women had been victims of attempted or completed rape.
- 82% of all juvenile victims are female.
- 90% of adult rape victims are female
- Females ages 16-19 are 4 times more likely than the general population to be victims of rape, attempted rape, or sexual assault
- Women ages 18-24 who are college students are 3 times more likely than women in general to experience sexual violence. Females of the same age who are not enrolled in college are 4 times more likely.
- 99,000 – number of perpetrators who will walk free.
- 1 out of every 6 American women has been the victim of an attempted or completed in her lifetime (14.8% completed, 2.8% attempted).

No, I wasn't in college, and to be honest, there isn't an exemption. But, the numbers are staggering. A lot went through my mind after the assault. I didn't see myself the same way again. I had so many questions, yet no one to share them with. I felt alone, scared, humiliated......ruined.

"I knew him." "He's my boyfriend, why would he do this to me?" "He took my virginity."

- 94% of women who are raped experience symptoms of post-traumatic stress disorder (PTSD) during the two weeks following rape.
- 30% of women report symptoms of PTSD 9 months after the rape.
- 33% of women who are raped contemplate suicide.
- 13% of women who are raped attempt suicide.
- Approximately 70% of rape or sexual assault victims experience moderate to severe distress, a larger percentage than for any other violent crime.

"Am I ruined?" "Am I stained?" "Tainted?" "How did I become a victim?"
Suicide? Suicide......suicide.............have I thought of suicide before? Yes, when I was in high school. It was the summer of my Senior Year in high school (we were living in Germany). I was in a lost place in my life. Teenagers go through that at times, right? For me, it was a cry for help (communication was not my strong suit in high school). My mom is in the U.S. to see about hip surgery, my sister and I were staying at a friend's until we knew what was going on with mom, but her dad didn't want us there, so we had to go someplace else. This person wanted us to clean her house for her, like we were maids. I was so stressed. But, this act that took place against my body, I didn't think suicide. I was more in shock of what happened. Trying to process it all in. I fell more into denial. I can understand why a woman would want to end her life. It's the stigma of being raped. The stigma that she is the rape. She feels as if that has become her identity.....the rape.....the assault. "What will people think of me?" "Will I be judged?" "Will I be blamed?" "How will I be treated?" Shame, guilt, embarrassment, and blame all flood her mind.....it did for me. I can see why a woman would contemplate

committing suicide. No, I do not condone it......but, I can understand it. At times, it seems better to keep it inside, and not tell anyone. I mean, if I were to report the rape, would there be proof? There was no blood. I didn't scream. I didn't fight. No proof of struggle. And.....his word against mine. Yes, I can understand the thought. There's an internal pain that takes place. One that none would understand. Stress begins to take over. I understand......

Some people fall into drugs:

- 3.4 times more likely to use marijuana.
- 6 times more likely to use cocaine.
- 10 times more likely to use other major drugs

I never thought of taking drugs. I've never been a smoker, and the closest thing to ever taking pills, were (are) vitamins. Then, I have to decipher how big the vitamins (it's a whole thing) are. But, I can see why. No, I do not condone the use of drugs at all, unless its doctor prescribed, and carefully monitored. Who wants to feel the pain of what took place. Someone takes away your right to say 'No' to having sex. Someone decides for you. For some women, it's an awful, violent situation (I have tears in my eyes).

Forced...brutally...emotionlessly...painfully...angrily....no   one should be subjected to this. Yet, in some minds, they believe this is okay. And, that THEY have a right to commit this act. What voice are they listening to? A 'No', is 'No'. For some women, they are coerced. It seems innocent, and then........what happened? If there was no struggle, was it really rape? Did she scream? Did I scream? I didn't struggle.....I didn't scream......does that make it okay? Again, when a violation takes place against one's body, there's the physical, but the internal and mental.....that's much deeper. Taking a drug will help the pain go away (lies from the enemy). Taking the drug can make the situation worse.

Sexual violence also affects victims' relationships with their family, friends, and co-workers:

- 38% of victims of sexual violence experience work or school problems, which can include significant problems with a boss, co-worker or peer.

- 37% experience family/friend problems, including getting into arguments more frequently than before, not feeling able to trust their family/friends, or not feeling as close to them as before the crime.
- 84% of survivors who were victimized by an intimate partner experience professional or emotional issues, including moderate to severe distress, or increased problems at work or school.
- 79% of survivors who were victimized by a family member, close friend or acquaintance experience professional or emotional issues, including moderate to severe distress, or increased problems at work or school.
- 67% of survivors who were victimized by a stranger experience professional or emotional issues, including moderate to severe distress, or increased problems at work or school.

I do have a question, or five, about these statistics. What if you're already having arguments with your family? A valid question, right? I personally, did not experience issues at work because of the.....crime (first time ever saying/typing/writing this). Just work itself was an issue for me. It was almost like, I was overwhelmed by work that I didn't have time to think about it. Again............denial. But, when a crime, like this, has been committed against one's body, it is easy to be.....distracted.....lost in thought.....wondering.......if it will cause problems at work or school because the focus is not on the work, it's focused on the crime. "Could this have been prevented?"

The getting into arguments with family and friends. This happens because, even though the woman did not ask for the crime to happen, a piece of the perpetrator has been left with her. If he was angry during the rape, anger will now be a part of her. If lying was a part of the perpetrator, lying will become a part of her. This is called, 'soul tides.' When you read the Book of 1 Corinthians, it speaks a lot about sex and being pure. *1 Corinthians 6:16* states, *"Do you not see and know that your bodies are members (bodily parts) of Christ (the Messiah)? Am I therefore to take the parts of Christ and make [them] parts of a prostitute? Never! Never! Or do you not know and realize that when a man joins himself to a prostitute, he becomes one body with her? The two, it is written, shall become one flesh [Genesis 2:24]." AMPC.* No,

I am not calling you a prostitute. I put these scriptures in here for a reason. Even during the rape, the two have become one. Which means, parts of you are in him (emotions, characteristics, etc....), and parts of him are in you. My ex-boyfriend used to lie quite a bit, so I would find myself lying more than I used to (yes, I used to lie.....). If the perpetrator was angry, then you'll become angry. "How could he do this to me?" The trust will be gone. You'll feel as if you cannot trust.....anyone because of the crime......the violation that took place. You'll feel isolated because of shame, guilt, embarrassment, blame, so you'll lash out at times without even realizing it. Because, you're hurting. "I'm hurting inside. I want to scream. I want to tell someone, but I am ashamed." Your trust is broken even more when the perpetrator was your boyfriend, friend, even....your husband. You thought you knew this person, and trusted that he would never hurt you. Oh, but the betrayal. The pain.....oh.....the pain. Physical pain, yes, but the mental and emotional pain.........oh, the pain. "My heart hurts." Depression may settle in, and your emotions, I mean, they will be all over the place. You're trying to grasp what took place, and you have so many questions. It can overtake your life, or......you can go into denial.

"Can everyone see?" Can they see that I've been raped?" "God, where were you?" I feel so guilty." "Was I raped?" I wasn't raped." "Where's the proof?" "Who will believe you, Danielle?" "Who?"

I read this statement from Joyful Heart Foundation (their website), "Sexual assault and rape are **never** a victim's fault. Sexual assault and rape are crimes motivated by a need to control, humiliate, and harm. **If a victim does not fight the acts, it does not mean consent.**" Am I a statistic? Am I a number?

REFERENCES

Rape, Abuse & Incest National Network (RAINN)
'Victims of Sexual Violence Statistics'
www.rainn.org

'Battlefield of the Mind Bible', Amplified Bible 2017 by Meyer, Joyce

REFLECTION

*"Why are you cast down, O my inner self? And why should you moan over me **and** be disquieted within me? Hope in God **and** wait expectantly for Him, for I shall yet praise Him, Who is the help of my countenance, and my God."*

*Psalm 42:11, AMPC **(emphasis added)***

Use this space to record your thoughts about the statistics you just read. Those were only a few. What are your thoughts? How are you feeling? Journal them here.

CHAPTER 5
DATING: THE SECRET

"O My God, I cry in the daytime, but You answer not; and by night I am not silent or find rest."

Psalm 22:2 AMPC

The rape took place on a Sunday, I heard from Jason Tuesday afternoon. He sent a text asking how I was doing, and that he missed me. That's what got me to respond back to him. He said that he missed me. I responded back that I was good (what I could muster up) and that I was at work. He wanted me to call him when I got off from work, so that he could hear my voice. Yep, that got me. He missed me and wanted to hear my voice. That almost made up for what happened. Did he not know what happened? Again, out of the two of us, why do I feel as if I am the only one bothered and shaken up from what happened? Maybe he'll bring it up when we talk later.

I called him on my way home from work (I know we are not to talk on the phone while driving, but....no excuse). I asked what he was up to, and he let me know that he didn't do anything all day because he was off. On Monday, he and some friends hung out. I wanted to scream at him through the phone, "APOLOGIZE FOR WHAT YOU DID TO ME!" "DON'T YOU KNOW WHAT YOU DID?" I couldn't get the words out...but I could get the tears out. I cried so hard silently, while tears streamed down my face, but I didn't want him to hear the tears. Why am I protecting him? He should hear my tears. This is all his fault. Right? Or, is it my fault? I am not going through this, again. I have to breakup with him. All of this is going through my mind while he is talking (I made sure to comment at times) and I am driving (I was paying attention to the road). This has to end. I pull up to my mom's house, and tell him that I was getting ready to go inside. Then, he asked me, "Can I see you tomorrow night?" I paused for a moment...it felt like an eternity, "Sure, I can stop by after work tomorrow. I just can't stay late." We hung up. I had a huge dread fall upon me, and with my head hanging low, I went inside the house.

Yes, I went to visit Jason after work the next day. I will be honest, I did not know what to expect. Remember that dreaded feeling I mentioned earlier, well, it was still there. It was as if, I couldn't shake the feeling. A part of me was nervous, a part of me was scared, a part of me was...what...angry...sad...lost...yes, a part of me was lost. I couldn't explain why I went to visit him. The place where the violation occurred, or do I call it a crime (that was still going through my head). His friends were there. Did he tell them? Do they know? If he did tell them, what exactly did he say? Will they try to rape me? Why am I here? Why can't I move...like...flee from this place? What is wrong with me? "Leave, Danielle. Get up and leave." That didn't happen. I did hangout for a few hours (as I mentioned before, my mom lived like an hour or so away, so I didn't want to get home late), and as I was heading out, Jason wanted to walk me to my car. I should say no, right? I allowed him to walk me to my car. He said that he was glad I came over, and wanted to kiss me goodnight. Should I let him? NO! Don't kiss him! I let him kiss me...why...I don't know...fear, maybe. I get in my car, and drive home. I need to end this. I can't stay in a relationship with him. It's like he's in denial that anything happened. I don't want to be in denial about what happened. Oh, God! What is happening? I don't understand what's going on. God, please help me...

I didn't hear from God...not that I would know because I barely took the time to get to know him (notice how I typed that). I felt like I didn't hear from God, because I was still with Jason. As the days started to turn into a couple of weeks, I forgot what happened. I forgot, but I always had a....what do you call it...it felt like....a heaviness....no...a foreboding spirit around me whenever I was with Jason. I was always expecting something bad to happen. The rape (still hard to say that, so I will just call it, 'The Secret') never came up, but I was allowing him to touch and kiss me. In fact, we were having sex. He wore a condom, but we were having sex. And, I was always going to meet him. After a month of the rape, I found myself staying the night at his place, which meant, we were going to have sex. I wasn't proud of it. I always felt...dirty. I found myself lying to my mom whenever I did stay at his place. That's that soul tide I was telling you about earlier. You see, Jason was good at lying. He always wanted to find ways to make more money, so he would go from job to job. He still worked at the hotel, but he wanted a side hustle as well. He and his friends would try to start side projects (that wouldn't go through). I would wonder, why am I with this guy?

By summer of 2007, I met Jason's dad and stepmom. They fell in love with me! They wanted to meet me, so we had dinner. They were like, "How did you get someone like her? She's too good for you. You don't deserve her." They turned to me, and were like, "Why are you with him?" I was asking myself the same question. We laughed it off, but it did stick with me. I wanted to tell them, 'The Secret', but would they believe me? What lies has he told them? Why do I want to cry? Why am I here? After dinner with his parents, we went back to his place, and.....had sex. I didn't stay the night, so I drove home, with tears streaming down my face. Why do I feel so cheap?

This became 'the norm' for the rest of the summer. I would hang out with him, and at times, stay the night. One weekend, I was at his place, and some of his friends were there. We were sitting on the couch, when he turned to me and said, "This is the longest I've been in a relationship. After a few months, I try to find something wrong with a girl so that I can break up with her. Or, do something so that she can break up with me. Maybe I need to try a little harder." I was wondering if 'The Secret' came to his mind. He said I was too perfect, and didn't fit into his world (did he think he was in the mafia?). I told him that I wasn't perfect. Even if I was, he ruined it. But, I couldn't say that part. I was at the point where I was like, "Okay, I am in a relationship. He still wants to see me. We have fun together. Right? "But, don't forget about 'The Secret.' That should've made you breakup with him. That showed who he really was."

I still wasn't telling people about Jason and me. Why wasn't I telling people about Jason? Was I embarrassed? I mean, if I was constantly feeling a foreboding spirit, shouldn't I tell someone about us....in case something happens? One of his friends had a condo in Sarasota (a really nice beach area in Florida). At first, Jason wanted me to go. Then, he changed his mind, and didn't want me to go. Why doesn't he want me to go? I realized that he was trying to break up with me, but I wouldn't let him. Why wouldn't I let him break up with me? I was pretty much forcing myself to go on this trip. Was there someone else? I couldn't let him go without me. I could tell that he wasn't happy about that, but I didn't care. When I put my foot down about going, he told me to find my own way there. WOW!! DID HE REALLY JUST SAY THAT?! But, why am I surprised about this? He showed his true colors before. Am I just going to overlook this, or say something? Say something...anything...

So...here I was on this weekend trip, with a guy who didn't want me there, yet I forced myself to be on this trip. Why? Afraid of missing out on the fun? Would there be any fun? Afraid that another girl/woman caught his eye? Should I care about that? Let's not forget, that none of my friends, nor my mom and sister, knew about this relationship. So, I am about two hours away from safety. If anything were to happen...who would know? No one, because of the soul tide....lying. I think I told my mom that my job had a weekend conference, or something like that (I was getting pretty good at this...but, was it worth it? And, did my mom know already?). By the way, I rode with him, his friend and his friend's girlfriend. It was awkward because I could tell he didn't want me there, and I think his friends knew as well, but I didn't care. He barely spoke to me on the way to Sarasota. He barely spoke to me once we arrived to the condo. It wasn't until that evening, he asked me if I wanted to walk out to the beach with him. Again, two hours away from safety, and it is dark outside. God, what am I thinking? Am I even thinking? He told me that he didn't want me to come on this trip (I figured that). That he wanted to get away from me (exactly....what did I do wrong?), but now he was happy I was here. What just happened? I am a little confused. Should I be mad? Should I be hurt? To be honest, I am not sure what I felt at that moment. I overlooked it, again. We went to bed that night, and I was good because I was with him...

The weekend was over and it was time to head back to Orlando. All seemed well for the next couple of weeks. We were planning a trip to Mexico to visit his mom. Well, this was exciting. Oh, did I mention that he said, "I think I love you?" No? Well, he did. I should've been thrilled, right? No, I wasn't. I told him that I felt the same way, but I didn't have any feeling behind it. Wasn't sure what that meant at the time. My response to him was....blech. One night, I was at his place, and we were talking. All of a sudden, he said he didn't want to do this anymore. What just happened? He said that this was getting too serious, and it wasn't what he wanted. WHAT...JUST...HAPPENED? This had to be a joke, right? I basically threw myself at this guy. Did the whole...clinging thing...lied for him...and he wanted to end this? Shouldn't I be happy? Shouldn't I want to be free? Free of him? NO! If we breakup, I won't have a boyfriend. That's what mattered, me having a boyfriend, not my freedom. We broke up. I left his apartment.

I drove home, with tears streaming down my face. Why am I upset about this? Remember 'The Secret'? Why am I having this reaction? This response? Don't forget about 'The Secret'...

It's been a month since Jason and I broke up. Why am I still sad? Now, it's been two months, and I think I am getting over Jason. An old friend from Colorado came down to Orlando so that we could go on a cruise. Not just any cruise, a Disney cruise. SN: They are the absolute best. Book one if you can, kids or no kids, they are the best. Back to the story. My friend and I stayed at the hotel that I worked at (still with the national rental car company) and....Jason still worked there. My friend, *Melissa knew about Jason (our relationship, not 'The Secret'), so when we pulled up to the hotel, I saw him and pointed him out to her. I walked by as if I didn't see him (I did). He tried to speak, but I acted as if I didn't notice (I did). Petty, I know, but I was still a little hurt from the breakup. Little FYI, Melissa and I had a great time on our cruise. Again, Disney is a must.

Thanksgiving 2007 comes and goes. Christmas 2007 comes and goes. I didn't think of Jason too much. In rolls 2008!!! I am still working for the national rental car company. How much longer do I want to wash cars....in the humidity....in pantyhose? Hmmm....Anyhow, one Saturday, I was walking around my neighborhood....my mom's neighborhood, when I received a phone call. Guess who it was? Jason. Why would he be calling me? It's been a few months. Now, I deleted his number when we broke up (back then, I was good with the CTRL + ALT + DELETE button. Once we stopped talking, I have to boot you out of the phone), but I still remembered his number. Has this happened to you? Anyhow, I answered the phone (why). He wanted to know how I was doing (did he really care). He said that he went to Mexico to visit his mom (the trip we were supposed to take together), and that he was missing me. He and his mom had a conversation about me. She asked him if he liked me, no, if he really cared about me, then he should call me and see about getting back together. He told me that while he was on the trip, he wished I was with him. Now, let me tell you something, I didn't jump up and down on this. I was very skeptical...I mean...just out of the blue, he calls me. I wasn't really buying into it. I told him that I wasn't sure about getting back together because he hurt me (the breakup), and I didn't want to deal with it again. I remember telling a co-worker about it, and he told me not get back together with Jason. He said something that shocked me, he said "You looked so sad and hurt when you guys broke up. You weren't your usual chipper self. I don't want you to go through that again." I had no idea that I looked that way. I thought I was hiding it pretty well, my feelings of the breakup. Hmmmm.....need to think about this.

Well, I thought about it....and.....Jason and I....got back together. I had a boyfriend, again! What's not to be excited about? We got back together in time for Valentine's Day 2008. He had a special night planned, so you know what that meant.......time to lie to my mom....again. It was the same 'ole, "There was a business meeting that was taking place, and I needed to stay the night at a hotel. The company was paying for it." Again, soul tides. Jason was good at lying, so I picked up on that. Right after work, I went to Jason's so we could spend Valentine's Day together. I was excited! I arrived at his place, and we kissed for a moment (no stirrings or anything). I wanted to show him the dress I was going to wear to dinner. It was a nice, white strappy dress. I had silver heels to go with it. I came out of the room with the dress on, and he liked it! He came over and started kissing me right away, then....moved me into his bedroom. Next thing, I am on the bed, he had a condom, and.......was it sex? After he was done, he got off of me, pulled up his shorts and left the room. I cried some. I felt so....cheap....so....dirty. I pulled myself together, and went out into the living room. We eventually left for dinner. It was good....I was on a date.....I had a boyfriend who had a special night planned for Valentine's Day. Why am I not excited anymore? After dinner, we went back to his place, and.......had sex. What am I doing to myself? Why did I get back with him? Because.....I have a boyfriend.......

Spring 2008 is here!!! It's that time of year to get my annual check-up. You know ladies, the Pap smear. Not my favorite thing in the world, but if it's to make sure that I stay healthy, then so be it. At this check-up, the Obstetrics and Gynecology (OB-GYN) saw something....found something. He saw a cyst on my ovary. WHAT?!? A CYST?! Before jumping to any conclusion, he wanted me to do an ultrasound (isn't that for when a woman is pregnant) to make sure it wasn't a cyst. He said that it was something pertaining to sex. He asked if I was sexually active, I said that I just recently became active. He asked if my partner had been with someone else. I didn't know if Jason had slept with someone else while we were apart. Should I be worried? I didn't share this with anyone, I mean, I wasn't telling anyone about Jason, so why mention this? The day came for the ultrasound. For the ladies who've been blessed to bear children, you know this means drinking 32 ounces (four glasses) of water. Shouldn't be a problem, right? Right, except you can't go to the bathroom before the appointment. Oh, did I mention that I was on my menstrual cycle? Well, I was, so.....this will be interesting. I know drinking all of the water helps to get a better view of what's going on inside, but if the nurse presses on my stomach one more time.....I will urinate on the table. It will not be pretty, but it's about to happen. How many more times does she need to press on my stomach? FINALLY...what seemed like hours (was only a few minutes), it was over. I was able to go to the restroom (thank you, Jesus). I would know in a few days of the results. As I lifted up a prayer to God (because that's what you do when you are dealing with an issue....and when you need like a BIG promotion, right), and asked him to heal me. Within a few days, I received a call. All was good, they just wanted to take the precautionary steps to make sure it wasn't anything serious...like...cancer. Whew!! Thank you, God!

After that was over.....things seem to be going well for Jason and me. I was staying at his place more, I was still trying to make this relationship....truly official...again. Then.....he decides he wants to breakup. WHAT?! WHY?!?! Why did I get back with him?! I am so angry at myself. I knew this would happen. Danielle, what's wrong with you? You knew better! I am screaming in my head!!! He gave some excuse for breaking up. I believe I tuned it out.....tuned him out....tuned us out. We weren't even back together six months, and we are breaking up....AGAIN! I would say that I deserve it. I am trying to make a guy be a man.....a gentleman......and it's not working. Remember what he did to you, Danielle? Do you remember? What was it again? Am I drawing a blank?

Late spring 2008 is here. I am sad that Jason and I are not together (please, do not ask me why). But, I am trying to stay positive. By doing this, I begin to read books about being motivated and being positive. I found myself drawn to books by Joyce Meyer and Joel Osteen. Books about changing habits and where every day should be a Friday. Let me tell you, none of this was a coincidence, but when you are not walking with the Lord, you don't catch it. This also means, that I need to look for another job. I found myself angry at times (not getting the sales that I needed), and I wasn't liking the fact that I had to work long hours, and not really have a weekend to reset. Things needed to change. Well, change was coming....or, sort of a change. Jason wanted back in the picture. I figured this time, I'd give him a hard time. Make him beg me to come back. Will it work...?

I was really focusing on getting a new job. Something that was more challenging for me. I mean, I learned a lot working for a national rental car company, but, I knew there was more. Plus, reading these books had me pulling out my Bible. Yeah, Joyce Meyer and Joel Osteen would have scripture in their books, so I figured I'd pull out my Bible to see what they were talking about. Again, I wasn't reading my Bible during this time, but nothing is ever really a coincidence. During my breaks at work, or when it was slow, I would read one of their books. One day, a gentleman came into the dealership to get his Cadillac looked at. I'd never seen him before. Some of the customers were repeats, but he was new. A sweet, gentle older man. He sat down in front of me (I remember him because he was friendly), and asked how my day was going. I told him well, but it could be better. While I was getting his paperwork together for his rental, he started to tell me about his wife. Actually, she passed away, and he was missing her. He said that she loved going to church and that he missed his best friend. That touched my heart. He asked if I was attending a church. I told him that I had not come across one. The few pastors that came through the dealership would invite me to their church, but I didn't like the way they looked at me, so I wasn't interested in going. He said he was sorry to hear that. He knew of a church and wanted me to come and visit. Something about this man made me feel at peace, and I felt that I could trust him. He gave me the name of the church, and I knew which church he was speaking of, location and all. He shared that the church had two services, 900 AM (traditional) and 1030 AM (contemporary). He said he attended the early service, and helped clean up behind the choir after first service. Oh man!!! I was getting excited. There was something about this man. His smile was warm. He was thoroughly interested in me. His tone was soft, warm and kind. I told him that I would love to attend church, and that I would look for him. He gave me the address to the church. Once we finished with the paperwork, I walked him to his rental car. He said he missed his wife, and didn't know how he was managing without her, but he said he did know who was helping him. I found myself saying, 'God is good." I hugged him and thanked him for inviting me to church. I told him to get home safe, and that I would see him on Sunday. As he drove off, I wished I had his number to check on him. Sunday arrived, and I was excited to go to church! I got up, took care of my health needs, got dressed and headed to church. I did attend the first service, and it was......different. The choir had their robes (hadn't seen that in a long time). The Pastor was friendly, knowledgeable and gave a sermon I could understand. After service, I stayed around to see if I could say 'hello' to the gentleman I met at the dealership a few days prior. I was greeted by a lot of people (friendly church), but couldn't find the gentleman. I finally asked an usher about the older gentleman that picks up behind the choir after service. She gave me this look.....like.....'huh?' She told me, "Honey, we don't have anyone that picks up behind the choir." I asked if she was sure because I met him a few days ago and he invited me to church. She said they never had anyone pick up behind the choir. I didn't believe her, so went I back inside to look for the gentleman. I hung around for about ten minutes, but, nothing. There wasn't anyone there. I was confused. I know this man existed because we talked for about 30-45 minutes at my job. Why wasn't he there? This boggled me all the way during my drive back home. I didn't get it. Very strange......how can someone invite you to church, but not be there? He wasn't a figment of my imagination. This was very strange......

After meeting the mysterious, sweet gentleman, I began to look for another job. Again, I needed a change. My uncle (my mom's brother) told me about a position of being a contract specialist for the ARMY. Hmmm...this would be something different. Monday-Friday, off on weekends, and look.....off on Government holidays. Consist of some traveling (I enjoy traveling). This would be something different. I filled out an application, submitted my resume and waited to see.....what....the.....Lord would do. Hmmm....I am calling on him now? Would he even help me? I mean, I wasn't calling on God often. It was only when I needed something. Anyhow, I need him now. I need a new job. Remember how I mentioned earlier about Jason? How he was trying to come back into the picture? Well, I was falling back into the trap.....the trap of wanting to be....no....having a boyfriend.....wanting to be with someone.....wanting to feel as if I was wanted. We were starting to hang out during the weekends.....correction....I was going to his place (he moved....he wasn't about stability). There was no compromising in this relationship, if that's what we're calling it. I was making sure not to go over and see him every weekend, I was beginning to feel needy. The times we did hangout, he wanted sex. Why was it always about sex? Couldn't we talk? Have a conversation....share our feelings? And, me, why do I keep coming back to this guy? Do I not know my worth? Am I this desperate? Whenever I would go home, I felt awful. I hated myself. I hated that I couldn't resist being around or near or with this guy. Why am I hanging onto him?

Well, I have some good news!!! I got the job!!! Yes, thank you, God! Now, it's time to give my two weeks' notice. The thing with national rental car companies (and this has been from first hand seeing this), two weeks notices were not always obliged. Now, let me tell you how this worked in my favor, and let's be real....it was God, but I didn't recognize this at the time. I met up with my Area Manager. Actually, he contacted me a week before to have lunch and talk. Well.....this new job came up during that week, so when I met with my Area Manager....I was nervous, but knew this needed to be done. Jesus, be a fence. I heard that somewhere before. I'm at lunch with my Area Manager and he proceeded to tell me how well I'm doing (remember that mouth I mentioned way earlier....it was still there. Learning to tame it). I knew where this was going. I was an Assistant Manager, and the next step would be to become a Branch Manager. Not something I was looking forward to, but it was nice to know that I was even thought of for such a position. After about 10 minutes of my Area Manager sharing the company's plans for me, he got quiet (it was my quiet that made him quiet). The next words out his mouth were, "You're leaving me, aren't you?" I told him yes. I received an offer for another job. He brought up the different ways that could keep me with the company. He asked who the job was with. I shared that with him, and he told me he couldn't compete with that. I handed him my letter of resignation. I told him I was aware that I may not fulfill the two weeks, if his manager said no. He told me that he would discuss with his manager and get back with me. He thanked me for my years with the company, and how he'd seen the changes and growth during our time of working with each other. He wished me well. Well, guess what?! I was able to work my last two weeks with the company. I kept expecting a phone call telling me that was my last day, but it never came. I was thankful to leave on a good note.

So, I shared the news with Jason. Look, I was trying to at least be friends with him. I believe we had dinner (he wanted to celebrate). I started my new job. The drive was even further than my previous job, but it was going to work out. Come to find out, Jason moved (again). This time, not too far from my job. He moved in with a friend and his girlfriend. Okay, well, what does this mean for us? Were we going to become a couple again? I didn't like being in limbo when it came to Jason. It always seemed that I was waiting for his approval, or his next move to determine where I would fit in. We played that game of going back and forth of being together, yet, weren't together. Now, I was not sexually active with anyone else, I am not sure if Jason was or not. I was getting better at saying 'no' whenever he wanted sex. He would get angry (again, showing his true colors), and didn't want to talk much if we didn't have sex. Clues I was not taking in.

2008 was coming to a close, and I was still messing around with Jason. It was like, 'Friends with Benefits' only, it was benefiting him if we had sex. You have to get out of this relationship, Danielle. Nothing about this is healthy for you. 2009 rolls in. This will be a different year. Little did I know that it would be just that? February of 2009, and I see that Joyce Meyer was coming to Orlando. You know, the one where I was reading her books about life changes? Yep, she was coming to Orlando, and it was free! I asked my mom if she wanted to go, she said yes. Friday rolls around, and I am excited to see Joyce Meyer. Mom and I arrive late (don't get me started), and we find seats near the top of the arena. After Joyce's teaching, she did an altar call (I later learned that this happens every time she has a conference. Friday nights are Altar Calls). She said that anyone that wanted to give their life over to Christ, and accept him as our Lord and Savior, to please stand. I stood right up. It was like....someone pulling me up. As she began to give us the words to receive Christ, I started crying. Tears were literally falling down my face. I said "Amen." Then, she said "For those who are already walking with the Lord, please welcome our new family members." I felt a hand on my right shoulder.....and....I....just....balled. It felt as if Jesus, Himself, was standing next to me and put His hand on my shoulder. I was a wreck!!! I was shaking uncontrollably. What was happening to me? Does this happen to others when they accept Jesus Christ into their lives? I remember looking to mom. Her face was frowned up as if to say, "Why are you accepting Jesus into your life?" I thought I did it all wrong. Maybe I didn't accept Jesus into my life correctly. What do I do? Do I do it again? I didn't harbor on it too much, because the woman behind me gave me a hug and welcomed me into the family. This was the woman whose hand was on my right shoulder. I told her thank you! Something amazing happened.....why did I want to share it with Jason? Once I got home, I called him and told him that I accepted Jesus into my life. He said, "Good for you", and moved on to something else. This was huge for me!!! I wonder what will happen next.

REFLECTION

"And I know I don't deserve this kind of love
Somehow this kind of love is who You are
It's a grace I could never add up
To be somebody You still want
But somehow
You love me as You find me."

'As You Find Me' by Hillsong UNITED

Those words are from one of my favorite worship groups, Hillsong UNITED. It speaks to exactly how I felt the moment I accepted Jesus Christ as my personal Lord and Savior. Still leaves me in complete awe. God wants me. What song (s) reveals your relationship with the Lord? The one, or two, that speaks to the depth of your soul, and wish you could say those exact words to God. God loves us where He finds us.

CHAPTER 6
THE BREAKUP:
This Needs to End

"BEHOLD, THE Lord's hand is not shortened at all, that it cannot save, nor His ear dull with deafness, that it cannot hear."

Isaiah 59:1 AMPC

So, I gave my life to Christ in February 2009. It was actually on my mom's birthday!! What do you think of that? This was so all new to me. I didn't really have anyone around to help guide me through this new chapter....season of my life. I did begin to attend church more regularly. In the beginning, it wasn't every Sunday. I found myself back with Jason, which meant, I was staying at his place more. Which meant, we were having sex (I cringe at this). I knew it was wrong before. I told myself that the one I gave myself to, would be the one I would marry. But..........by the Spring of 2009, I made some friends at work, so a few of us wanted to hangout after work for Happy Hour (why is it called 'Happy Hour' if you are drinking your cares away?). We met at a popular sports bar, The Ale House, and some of my co-workers met Jason. I was excited for them to meet Jason, again, because I was in a relationship, I felt important......worthy.....that I was somebody. Something seemed off, but I couldn't quite put my finger on it. I don't have a problem talking and laughing it up with people. I also have a tendency to check in on those around me to make sure they are comfortable. Jason wasn't comfortable, and my co-workers (the guys) weren't really talking with him either. I remember one of my co-workers ask my future boss what did he think of my boyfriend? He said he didn't care too much for him. Something about him that he didn't like. Hmmm.......that caught me off guard. Jason wasn't around to hear that, at least, I don't think he was. That was......interesting.

June 2009 rolls around, and my maternal grandmother is not doing well. She's the one I lived with while attending Southern University. Our mom went to Louisiana to see how grandmother was doing. After about a week, our mom told us (my sister and I) that she was in the hospital. There was talk of amputating her legs. Grandmother was getting dementia. She had healthcare workers to stay and watch over her at her home. It was getting to the point to where she could barely walk, and she was in pain. Now, she's in the hospital. My sister and I planned to go and spend a week in Louisiana. We were going to drive (translation....I was going to drive) there. If you leave ly enough, you can make it in a day. I shared the news with Jason. Maybe I was looking for so much, you know, the "Oh, babe. I am sorry to hear about your grandmother. Is there anything I can do for you? Do you need anything?" I didn't get that. Not even close. My sister and I made it on a Saturday. Grandmother seemed to be up in spirit. Mom looked a bit tired. During the day, we'd spend it at the hospital (my mom, sister and I). During the evenings, my uncle (mom's younger brother) would stay at the hospital, and the three of us would sleep at grandmother's. Grandmother was alert. She knew we were there. She would still fuss at us and the nurses.....only grandmother. I would call Jason to let him know what was going on, but he didn't seem interested. He's supposed to be my boyfriend, and want to know how I was doing. I found myself calling my friend, Melissa (my cruise friend) a lot and sharing updates with her. Why wasn't Jason calling me? Then, it came time for grandmother to have her legs amputated (up to her knees). A decision my uncle made, but one I don't think my mom was keen on. Grandmother went in alert, but she came out of the surgery......different. And, I am not meaning because of her loss of limbs, but......she just didn't seem right. I am not a fan of hospitals, I don't believe anyone really is. It's cold, dreary, a lot of beeping machines, nurses and doctors coming in and out of the rooms, oxygen bags....I mean, I know good can come from being at the hospital, birth of a child (or two), a life-saving surgery, but hospitals are not my thing. I was all ready to leave, but wanted to see my grandmother and my mom. Once back in her room, my grandmother.....did I mention she seemed different? I wasn't expecting her to be talkative right out from her surgery. But, the next day, I wasn't seeing movement. I remember telling my mom that grandmother didn't look good. Mom thought it was due to the surgery, but I knew it was something different. I was beginning to feel saddened because I felt as if she wouldn't make it. Each day, it seemed as if she was getting worse. Her breathing was.....haggard. It was as if she was struggling to breathe. "Oh, that's normal." No, it wasn't. She wasn't eating. Was anyone seeing this? After the third day, I think my mom was beginning to see it, her mom was not recovering like they hoped. "Come on, God. Can't you save my grandmother? You see the pain it's causing my mom, to watch her mom beginning to dwindle away. Where are you, God?" I, personally, could not handle watching my grandmother dwindle away, and watch my mom watch her mom....dwindling away. I had to get back to work, so my sister and I left to go drive back to Florida on a Saturday. I just wanted to get away. I didn't want to watch this anymore. During all of this, I didn't really hear from Jason, but I didn't care. I was losing my grandmother. My sister and I made it back pretty late. We called mom to get an update about grandmother, and how she (mom) was doing.

Sunday evening, we receive a phone call. It's mom, and she doesn't sound well. She asked how we were doing (trying to make small talk), I asked what was wrong (I could tell by the sound of her voice). "Grandmother passed away today. Not too long ago." WHY?!?! WHY, GOD?!?! My sister and I were both on the phone, so we heard the news together. We just balled. We just lost what we knew Louisiana to be, our grandmother. To take a trip to Louisiana meant visiting grandmother. It was as if, Louisiana only existed because of grandmother. We asked how she (mom) was doing, she was in shock. She said she would call us back about funeral arrangements. Funeral arrangements?! Already?! Mom said it would be easier being that her and her brother (our uncle) were already in there. I called Jason after I hung up with my mom. Again, was I expecting too much from my boyfriend? He didn't seem to have any cares. He just said he was sorry to hear the news. I quickly called my friend, Melissa, and told her. I cried on the phone with her. I called Maria, too. Remember her? She's the sweet friend who allowed me to stay with her when Eric and I broke up back in Colorado. She also let me cry on the phone. I went in to work that Monday (to get my mind off of the loss of my grandmother). I told my Supervisor and some co-workers what happened. Mom called me that afternoon to let me know that the funeral would be on Friday. Like, Friday of this week. So soon....okay, I need to request more leave. I wasn't hearing much from Jason, but I needed to focus on my family. My sister and I head back to Louisiana. We left on a Wednesday. Had Thursday to help out and prepare, and then....Friday came. I was feeling so bad. I wasn't the best granddaughter. I kind of had a rebellious stage in my early twenties. I was thankful that my grandmother allowed me to stay with her during my college years, but I did have a mouth (remember, I mentioned that earlier). God, did she know that I loved her? I don't think I showed her that I loved her. So many regrets and anger at myself. I wish I had more time with her. God, I ask for forgiveness with how I treated my grandmother. I could've been more grateful and obedient. Why am I such an awful person? Is this what it's like to start talking to God? This is new for me. The funeral went well. We celebrated grandmother's life (she would've loved all of the attention). We wore white, not black. I didn't have time to grieve because I was watching my mom's every move. If she needed to cry, I wanted to be her shoulder. She was hungry, I would make her plate. I knew she was tired. In a span of two weeks, my mom watched her mom be in high spirits, then......lose her. I was there for my mom, but, Jason wasn't there for me. I wasn't checking my phone every two minutes, but the times I did check my phone.....no missing phone call from Jason. Not even a text. I was hearing from other friends (thankful for them), but not from my boyfriend. Back to the family, my sister and I left Louisiana the following Tuesday to get back to work. Our mom stayed until that Friday. This was a tough time (one of the toughest) in my life, and.....where.....was.....Jason? I am not understanding this. Again, am I asking for too much from my boyfriend? Why am I with this guy? So, 2009 started with me accepting Jesus into my life, getting back with Jason and then losing my grandmother by June. What else is to happen this year?

July is my birth month, so I always celebrate for the entire month (just a little side note). I like to have dinner with friends, go to the beach, and go to the amusement parks, pretty much I just enjoy celebrating (I like to do the same for my friends too). Jason and I are still......we're still seeing each other. The weekend before my birthday, a few of my co-workers and I went out to dinner. I wanted a 'Girls Night Out' with good food, music and laughter. My mom and sister also took me out to eat that weekend (I also like to eat). On the day of my birthday, Jason and I went to Disney World. Back then, you were able to get into the park for free on your birthday. I am not sure if they do that anymore. Jason was also able to get a free ticket to the park (please do not ask me how), so we spent the day at the park, riding the rides, trying to be a couple, but I was having fun at the park. It had been years since I've been to Disney World. Later that evening, Jason took me out to a nice fancy dinner. I felt special, but....empty. A part of me knew this wouldn't last, but I was going to enjoy the moment, if that's what this were to be. Remember, I mentioned that he moved, so he wanted me to stay the night at his new place (he was actually rooming with two other women). I remember telling him no, and that I had to get home.

His mood changed. It kind of scared me. I wasn't sure if he would try to attack me, physically and/or sexually. He did calm down, but on my way home, I was thinking, "What just happened? Am I not to say no? Why am I in this relationship?"

A couple of weeks before my birthday, I had my annual check-up. I received a phone call from the OB-GYN stating that I needed to come in. The next day, after work, I head over to the OB-GYN. I was told that they found something on my cervix. Right there, I was told that they had to take some tests over the next few weeks. What?! At this moment, they would have to scrap some tissue from my cervix to send to the laboratory. What?! I am in a daze at this point. I had to get back on the table, and let them scrap some tissue from my cervix. I had to make an appointment for the next check-up, which would be in two weeks. WHAT IS HAPPENING?! I drove home in shock (in Florida, there is so much traffic, so I had time to stay in shock and recover before getting to mom's). Two weeks later, I am back at the OB-GYN. This time, they are going to ice my cervix, and snip a piece to send to the lab. I felt that snip, and it hurt. All I could do was cry. There was a little bleeding. I wasn't crying because of the snip, I was crying because of what I was going through. Why is this happening to me, God? Did I do something wrong? After the icing and snipping, I got myself together. The doctor told me why this was happening.....they think they see signs of cervical cancer, and they want to make sure that it doesn't turn into that. Cervical cancer......me.......cervical cancer......me.......cervical cancer.......this keep going through my mind while the doctor was talking. He said that I had a Sexually Transmitted Infection (STI), which was Human Papillomavirus (HPV). Typically, the male carries this infection, but doesn't shows any symptoms. And, if he's had multiple sex partners, this puts you more at risk. There were no signs of bleeding after sex, nor pain during sex. I would not have known had I not had my annual a month before. WHAT?! I cannot believe this!!! But, can I believe it? This is the second time that my health has been at risk due to me being careless with Jason. When I say careless, I mean just by being with him. Oh my goodness!!! What happens now? Once they receive all of the results, they would contact me and let me know. The doctor was pretty certain they got all of it. I left the office, and sat in my car, and cried. "God, why is this happening to me? Did I do something wrong? Do you not love me? I'm so scared.

I don't want to have cervical cancer. God, please help me." On my way home from the doctor, I called Jason. There was this feeling that I needed to stop by his place, and tell him what was happening. *You'll see why.* Where did that come from? It was fleeting, so I didn't really pay any more attention to it. But, whose voice was that? Anyhow, I made it to Jason's. He wanted to hug me when I came in, but I felt an arm hold me back. I calmly begin to inform Jason what was going with me. How I had my annual check-up, what the doctor found, and what I had endured. His response, "What does this have to do with me?" WHAT DID HE SAY?! What did he mean what does this have to do with him? I explained that the doctor found a STI, and that it could turn into cervical cancer. He wasn't concerned at all. He said I didn't get it from him. He is the only guy I've had sex with! I explained (again) how the male can carry the trait for HPV, but show no symptoms. He kept denying that this was possible. How could he not show any symptoms? Is he not listening to me? He didn't ask how I was doing. He didn't ask if I was in any pain. His concern was on him, and how he didn't have any symptoms, so I didn't get this from him. I asked if he assumed I slept with someone else. He asked if I did. Let me tell you, the inside of me jumped and wanted to....to.....hit him......knock him out (being honest). I was so angry. But, something......someone.......was holding me back. It felt as if there someone actually holding my arm, and restraining me from trying to get to Jason. What was happening? Why can't I get to him? I want to wipe that smirk off his face. I told him that I was a virgin when we met, so there was no one else I had been with (sexually....all the way). He asked, "Who would be a virgin in their 30s" I told him me! He didn't believe me. He said it couldn't be true. Didn't something happen when we first started dating? He's killing me from the inside out. Can't he see that? This isn't fair. Before it got into a screaming match, Jason FINALLY offered to go with me the next time I had a doctor's appointment. Mind you that it's been 30 minutes, and now he asks if he can accompany me to the doctor's. Again, in my mind, I am screaming at him. I told him no. God's been with me since this started, and he will be with me until the end. Where did that come from? He tried to give me a hug, but I didn't want a hug. I wanted an apology, but......that wasn't happening. He said he would get checked out. He had a friend that could take some tests (did he think he was part of the mafia?). I told him he could do what he wanted, and then I left. *You'll see why.* I understood why I had to go to Jason's. I truly needed to see his heart. He didn't care about me. He never cared about me. I was seething driving back home (please do not ever drive angry). I, of course, had to be calm before getting to my mom's because, she doesn't know any of this. I don't need her asking me questions. I wasn't ready to answer them. God, what do I do?

The answer came about a week later. I was out with a few friends, and it hit me to call Jason. We hadn't spoken much since the......what would you call it......the argument at his place. I called him, and told him that we needed to talk. He agreed. We just needed to pick a day. The next day, I happened to check my emails, and saw one from him. What is this about? I am honestly trying not to laugh, but Jason was trying to break up with me first, and via email. Oh no!!! I didn't even finish reading his email before calling him. I told him that he was going to be a man, and not hide behind the computer. It wasn't about who was going to do the breakup first, but it would be done in person. He was quiet at first (I did come off kind of strong, but it was going to be done correctly), then he agreed. We picked to talk on a Friday (Labor Day Weekend was coming up). He called me Thursday to let me know that he picked up a shift Friday, so we wouldn't be able to meet. Okay, that makes sense. So, we moved our meeting to Saturday. Friday night comes, and he calls to tell me that he picked up a shift for Saturday. Is he trying to avoid this talk? I told him that we needed to meet and not procrastinate about this. This relationship truly needed to end. Monday was Labor Day, and I called Jason to let him know that I was on my way over so that we could talk. I arrived at his place, and............here we go. I told him that this relationship was not a healthy one. My life had been in danger a couple of times (not counting the secret that took place), and he didn't care. I told him that I don't think he ever loved me. We were blocking each other's blessings. I told him that God has an amazing man for me. One who would appreciate me, treat me with respect and be in awe that God placed us in each other's lives. I believed that the same would happen to him. That God would bring him a woman that he would cherish. This was it. This was goodbye. These were his following words, "Can we have goodbye sex?" WHAT?!?!?! Did he really just say that? He said he was joking, but he was serious. I didn't respond, I just turned around, walked out the door, and never looked back. On the way home, I was feeling......relief......anger......hurt........broken. Why am I feeling this way?

CHAPTER 7
WHOSE VOICE AM I
LISTENING TO?

"[Inasmuch as we] refute arguments and theories and reasonings and every proud and lofty thing that sets itself up against the [true] knowledge of God; and we lead every thought and purpose away captive into the obedience of Christ (the Messiah, the Anointed One),"

2 Corinthians 10:5, The Amplified Bible (AMPC)

"Think about the things of heaven, not the things of earth."

Colossians 3:2, NLT

"Be well balance (temperate, sober of mind), be viligiant *and* cautious at all times; for that enemy of yours, the devil, roams around like a lion roaring [in fierce hunger], seeking someone to seize upon and devour."

1 Peter 5:8, AMPC (emphasis added)

So, September 2009, Jason and I broke up. I wasn't going back to him. Even if he tried to sweet talk me, by saying he missed me, I wasn't going back to him. Why do I feel....lost.....broken.....used......rejected? I didn't like this feeling, but I can disguise it. I've been pretty good with doing that, disguising how I really felt. I didn't feel like answering questions, or hearing the "I told you so", even though, no one told me. At times, it's AFTER the breakup that your friends, or family, have something to say about the relationship. You know, "You were too good for him." "I didn't like him anyway." "I knew he wasn't for you." I heard all of these when Eric and I broke up. That, honestly, does not make the person feel better. It actually makes them feel worse. As if, they are the WORST person in the world because of the relationship they were in. That's how I was feeling once Eric and I broke up, because people had their comments. Our words mean a lot, and when taken in, they can cause one to go into depression, have suicidal thoughts, and more. I understand that family and friends care, but throwing out comments like, "I didn't like him anyway", or "I knew he wasn't for you," doesn't make it better. I didn't have suicidal thoughts or go into depression when Eric and I broke up, but I could feel myself going into depression when Jason and I broke up. It didn't happen right away.

Made some new friends at work, so I was going out a bit more. Nothing heavy, more like comedy clubs, dance clubs (I like to dance), going to the movies, and going out to eat (food is a love language of mine). I did go out drinking once (can I be honest). A co-worker had free tickets to like a.....ummmmm.....a karaoke bar. She invited quite a bit of us, so we all went out that Friday night. I will be honest, I had a good time. Not because of a few drinks, but the laughter....I needed the laughter. I just knew I had to be careful with not over drinking....because.....I've heard stories.....and when Jason and I first broke up, I wanted to go down this path. But, something prevented me from doing so. Well, Halloween was around the corner, and a co-worker had a Halloween Party, and I invited a few friends that I used to work with at the national rental car company. One of them (*David) told me he saw Jason downtown the weekend before (I wasn't looking forward to this at all). They bumped into each other, and Jason acted as if he wanted to fight, then he remembered David (we all went to the club for my birthday a few months earlier). David asked Jason how were things between us (he didn't know we broke up before seeing him). Jason told him that we weren't together anymore. David was surprised to hear that. He asked Jason what happened. Jason didn't want to talk about it. He told David it didn't end well, and that he was still taking it pretty hard. That surprised me, but I didn't show it. David asked if I was doing well, and I told him I was good. He didn't press (thank you, God), but said if I need anything to let him know. Jason's name was not mentioned the rest of the night. I didn't even think about him on my way home.

Hey 2010! Welcome! I started attending church more. Second service worked for me because of the contemporary style of music. Nothing against the traditional, but my spirit connects with music on different level. Since accepting Jesus into my life in 2009, I found myself trying to listen to Christian music. So, I had this thing; Mondays-Saturdays, secular music and Christian music on Sundays (sounds about right. Sunday is God's day, right?). Now, at second service, we would sing songs, and I was feeling them. Our God is Greater....oh my goodness! The choir knows how to write songs! It would take me about 45 minutes to an hour to get to church, but I was going to make it every Sunday. I had my Bible from high school. Whenever the Pastor would teach, I would feel a nudge...a tap in my spirit. What is this? Why do

I feel a......stirring? What is this about? I didn't really have anyone to ask about these feelings, and why they were coming about. So, I kept them to myself. Now, also I would feel a nudge whenever the Pastor would ask if anyone wanted to be baptized. This nudge became more prominent after Jason and I broke up. I would think, "Yes, if the Pastor asks about baptizing today, I will do it." Then, it would turn into, "Well.....I just got my hair done yesterday. So, next week." Then, the following week would come, "I mean, I am in a dress today. So, next week." Each week I had an excuse, and the nudging's wouldn't go away. What is this about?

Well, as mentioned in this chapter, 'Welcome 2010!' Let me tell you, the nudging's about this baptism were not going away. Okay, God.....what do you want me to do? Next thing I know.......I am filling out a card and checking that I want to be baptized! How did this happen? The date picked, January 30, 2010.....a Saturday. (I remember the date because the following Sunday was Super Bowl, and the Indianapolis Colts were going to be in the game). I received a letter in the mail, and a phone call. This was impressive. The day before I got baptized, I shared with my mom that I would be getting baptized. She was upset......because.... I didn't tell her sooner so that she could invite people. To be honest, I just wanted this to be my moment. And, I didn't want my uncle there (he and I weren't speaking too much due to the assault some years prior). And, I wanted to think about what I was doing. Probably selfish of me, but I didn't have a strong relationship with my mom, so I didn't want her there either. That Saturday, I arrived at the church. It was evening that they were doing the baptisms. I get upstairs, and there were pastors waiting for me. I had a change of clothes for the baptism. I don't remember their names, but they were so kind and thoughtful. Next person to walk in the room....the Pastor, himself. Now, I knew he was tall, but I didn't know he was that tall. He gave me a hug (again, he is tall), and told me how proud he was of me, and that he'd been praying for me. This was exciting, and that the heavens were rejoicing. Oh wow!!! That took my breath away. Then, he and the others prayed over me. I started crying (wasn't sure why). Next thing you know, I am walking towards the....water (I wanted to say the pool because that's what it looked like). I am in the water.....cold water. The pastor (not the lead Pastor) asks me if this is what I wanted to do. Allow my old self to wash away, and come up clean, and declare Jesus as my Lord and Savior (I am paraphrasing). I said yes. He dunked me in the water, and I came back up. I heard people cheering for me, and I started.....crying. He congratulated me and welcomed me into the family. I went back to the room to change. As I was heading home, I was trying to process what all just took place. I made a big decision in my life. I did it earlier in 2009, when I accepted Jesus into my life. Now, I was declared 'clean' because of what Jesus did for me. This was mind-blowing! Now what?

Well, after a couple of months of being baptized, I finally decided to fill out the card. You know, the one in front of the pew that is in front of you. Who doesn't try to avoid those? But, I felt a nudging (what is with the nudging) to fill out the card. So, I did, begrudgingly. I checked the box wanting to join like a Bible Study Group......something like that. I wasn't expecting a phone call, so I was surprised when I received one from the church (they actually call you?). The administrator told me of a Bible study group. It was a singles group. They still discussed the Bible, but also had outings each month. This group was led by the Singles Pastor (except, he wasn't single). Okay, this was new for me. I figured I'd give it a shot. What's the worst that can happen? My first Sunday, and I arrive....kind of excited. Not knowing what to expect. I'm greeted, and my name is on a list (am I like V.I.P.?). Right away, I noticed that there were more single women than men. No, I was not looking to meet a guy, but too many women......sometimes, that's not a good thing. There can be pettiness, gossiping (can I be honest?), cliques.....not sure I wanted to do this. I never really hung around a lot girls because of the reasons I mentioned. But, I figured, because its church it would be different. Oh, I forgot to mention. There weren't too many African Americans in this group (what emoji face do I enter here....). I've been used to it all of my life, but.....come on. No black people attend this church? What am I doing here? I will say, the group was nice. You know when you're the 'new kid' in school, and everybody wants to be the 'first' to introduce themselves, or be your new friend? It was like that. But again, the people were nice. So, I was baptized a couple of months earlier, now I am attending a Bible Study Group.....I believe they were called Small Groups. A few of the ladies already wanted to hang out, and they told me of another group, or Bible Study meeting for singles. This would be on Tuesday nights. Okay, I will think about it (moving too fast here, everybody be calm). The Singles Pastor was a great teacher. The way he taught was helping me to understand the Bible a bit more (learning where these books are, who the people are, etc.....). He made me want to return to the class, because I wanted to learn more about Jesus and what I mean to Him.

Spring 2010, I am connecting a bit more with some of the ladies of the Small Group. Starting to read The Bible a bit more. I still have a lot to learn, but this is good. Small steps. I happen to jump on Facebook one day, and Jason came across my feed (yes, we were still 'Friends' on Facebook, but I wasn't stalking his pages). He moved to Vegas to be near his mom (they were close). Well, I noticed that he was in a relationship. OH!!! And, he made it known. When he and I were together, he didn't have any postings of us. Was he embarrassed of our relationship? Was it because of my race? That I was older? I decided to 'Hide' his page, so that he wouldn't come through my feed. I will admit, that it bothered me a little. Was I a secret? I may not have told my mom, but I did tell some friends about him. He couldn't do that with me? I was starting to become angry, so I buried it in me. Hanging out with some of the ladies from the Small Group was helping me to not think or focus on Jason. I still felt awkward around them, like I couldn't be.....me, but it was helping me to not fall into depression.

Hey, Summer 2010!!! My birthday is around the corner, and I planned a trip to Vegas with a couple of friends. One day, I was playing Mafia Wars on Facebook (that was my addiction when I first started with Facebook). A message popped up. Wait? Who is this?

Jason? Why is he contacting me? Now, he didn't write a message on my 'Wall', it was the DM. I didn't like that. I didn't answer right away. I acted as if I didn't see it, plus I was playing Mafia Wars. After 20 minutes, I responded. The conversation went like this:

Jason: Hey. How are you?
Me: Good. What's up?
Jason: I just wanted to say hi.
Me: Hey
Jason: What are you doing?
Me: Playing a game.

Danielle Cador

Jason: Have you been out to Vegas yet?
Me; No, going for my birthday.
Jason: Do you have plans for when you come out here?
Me: (Is he for real?) Yep. A lot planned.
Jason: Do you think we could meet up? I'd like to see you.
Me: (IS HE FOR REAL?) Every day I have something planned, so I don't think I'll have time.
Jason: Can you make a night for dinner?
Me: Will your girlfriend be joining us?
Jason: ....No.
Me: No, we cannot meet up. I have too much planned. Plus, it's disrespectful to ask me out to dinner knowing that you have a girlfriend. And, it's disrespectful that you are sending me a private message. I respect your girlfriend, so this conversation is ending.

I don't know if he ever wrote back, but I went back to playing my game. The nerve of him. Asking me to meet him. That was a trap, I was not falling back into. I went on my trip to Vegas, and was hoping that Jason would not try to contact me. Thank goodness, he didn't. I had a good time with a couple of friends. Just have to remember. Vegas......July.....very hot. Not to do that again.

Well, 2010 was coming to an end. I wasn't reading my Bible as much as I should've been. I would write in my journal at times. I would lift up prayers to God, but I wasn't spending time with him like I knew I should be doing. I wonder if God is upset with me for not spending more time with him. 2011 was here. Wow!! 2010 went by fast. I am still attending church, as well as the Small Group. I actually did decide to attend the Singles Group on Tuesday nights. The Singles Pastor was leading this group as well. Being who I am, I went from just attending on Tuesday nights, to being a greeter. How did this happen? To be honest, I am not surprised because of my upbringing (being a military brat). I like to meet and connect with people. So, I wasn't surprised that I found myself going from just an attendee, to a greeter. Again, the Singles Pastor's teachings were helping me to stay in the Bible. I told myself that in 2011, I would start to read the Bible more, not just when attending church or Small Group. I would also take notes. I was definitely doing this. I was learning more of who God is. And, that He (learning) deserves to be praised and respected being that He is

Sovereign (still needed to learn this). We are not to bring God to our level, this meant that God was not 'he', but 'He'. Now, this was mind-blowing to me because I was definitely bringing God to my level, and I wasn't realizing it. I was feeling bad, but was also learning that God doesn't hold that against us. He is a forgiving God (I will have to look that up), and loving (He really loves me?). Learning more about God was starting to get exciting. After the sessions.....meetings....teachings (not sure what to call it), I would tell the Singles Pastor that his discussions and teachings were helping me stay in the Bible more. I was still hanging out with some of the ladies in the Small Group, but......something was off. Stay alert, Danielle.

Speaking of staying alert, in February 2011, I decided to fast. Now, I do not know what made me do this because I didn't really know what fasting was about. I mean, I've heard of fasting, but didn't know the importance of fasting. Are they really 21 days? Who does a fast for 21 days? I am to completely stop eating (food is a love language for me)? I had questions....but still decided to fast (please do not ask me why). My fast started on February 1, 2011. On February 14th (a Monday), Valentine's Day, my mom and I made plans to go see a movie. No, I did not get popcorn, but I definitely wanted to. I happened to check Facebook (not sure why). I saw that I had a message. Who could this be? It was Jason. What's going on? I haven't heard from him since last year, why am I hearing from him now? Well, I was about two weeks into my fast, and what I did not know (by do now), is that Satan will try to tempt you during your weakest moments. When you study the Gospel, you'll read that Satan did this with Jesus. If you go to the Book of Matthew, chapter 4 verses 1-11, you can read and see how Satan *tries* to tempt Jesus. Here it is:

'Then Jesus was led by the Spirit into the wilderness to be tempted there by the devil. For forty days and forty nights he fasted and became very hungry. During that time the devil came and said to him, "If you are the Son of God, tell these stones to become loaves of bread." But Jesus told him, *"No! The Scriptures say, 'People do not live by bread alone, but by every word that comes from the mouth of God.'"* Then the devil too him to the holy city, Jerusalem, to the highest point of the Temple, and said, "If you are the Son of God, jump off! For the Scripture say, 'He will order his angels to protect you. And they will hold you up with their hands so you won't even hurt your foot on a stone.'" Jesus responded, *"The Scriptures also say, 'You must not test the Lord your God.'"* Next the devil took him to the peak of a very high mountain and showed him all the kingdoms of the world and their glory. "I will give it all to you," he said, "if you will kneel down and worship me." *"Get out of here, Satan,"* Jesus told him. *"For the Scriptures say, 'You must worship the Lord your God and serve only him.'"* Then the devil went away, and angels came and took care of Jesus.' – New Living Translation (NLT) *emphasis* added.

I was 14 days into the fast......and it was Valentine's Day.......and the flesh was getting weak. Should I open the message? No, I shouldn't. Should I? I did. I wanted to see what he wrote, not so much wanting to get back with him. I actually did not want to get back with him. I wasn't even missing him. But, I still wanted to see what he wrote. In his message (it was pretty long) he stated how much he missed me. I will paraphrase the message. He was thankful that I came into his life, and that I was a blessing. He said I taught him quite a bit (not sure what I taught him). He missed me being a part of his life, and wanted to be friends. There was more, but that was the jest of the message. I didn't respond to the message. Did I want to be friends with him? Did I need him back in my life? On Tuesday (the 15th of February), I attended the Singles Group. After the teaching, I asked the Pastor if I could speak with him. I shared with him (as much without getting into too much detail) about Jason. I told him about the message I received from Jason. The Pastor asked if I responded to the message. I told him no. He asked me the following questions, "If you allowed him back into your life, could you say that you guys would just remain friends? And, do you want him back in your life?" Okay, Pastor. Being real with the questions. None of my friends had asked me these questions (maybe they were afraid to.....just trying to give the benefit of the doubt). I answered, "No" right away. And, it was to both questions. He told me not to respond to the message. If I did respond, it would open up doors that I didn't need open. That was so good!! I actually deleted the message when I got home. Man!! That was a test....a struggle....a dilemma. None of which I wanted. Okay, 7 more days of this fast. Lord, carry me through.

The Butterfly Effect

In April 2011, I received some news from work. It was coming close to completing the intern program, and they were actually going to move it up a bit, so the class would be finishing a few months earlier. Oh wow!!! That's awesome news! I wouldn't be completing the program with my co-workers. What? I was going to be held back a year. What? This was told to me privately. All of the interns were called into a room and told that they would be completing the program early. I was told to wait because there was a 'special project' I would be working on. After everyone left, that's when I found out that I would be held back. Oh my goodness! What does this mean? I went back to my office, and held a poker face (I can be good at that at times). It was on the way home that I started crying. "Why is this happening to me, God? Did I do something wrong? Are you angry with me?" Nothing. I didn't hear anything. I was devastated. I was embarrassed. I was hurt. I was angry. WHY ME???? I couldn't tell my mom. What would she think of me? What does God think of me?

Driving to work the next morning, I was in pain.....mentally and emotionally. "Everyone knows that you've been held back. They are going to look at you with such disdain. If God loved you, why would he allow this to happen to you?" This is what I heard in my mind on my way to work. "Why, God? Why did You allow this to happen to me? Why me?" "*Why not you?*" Where did that come from? And, my question wasn't answered. "Why me?" "*Why not you?*" What's going on here? I just started crying. "I can't do this, God. What am I to do?" I was listening to Z88.3. It's a Christian radio station here in Orlando. The next song in their rotation was 'Praise You in This Storm' by Casting Crowns (side note: I used to get them and Third Day mixed up). I may have heard the song here and there, but not the full song. If you haven't heard this song before, these are the lyrics to the chorus:

And I'll praise You in this storm
And I will lift my hands
That You are Who You are
No matter where I am
And every tear I've cried
You hold in Your hand
You never left my side

And though my heart is torn
I will praise You in this storm

I completely broke. Tears were just streaming down my face. Didn't I just fast? I thought I had my struggle. That's not how it works. Not when walking with the Lord. Oh, now the bridge to the song comes up:

I lift my eyes unto the hills
Where does my help come from?
My help comes from the Lord
The Maker of Heaven and Earth

Okay, this song is tearing me apart. The words were cutting my heart. I arrive to work (by the grace of God). I had to pull myself together. With my head hanging low, I walked into my building. I did feel as if everyone knew, and they probably did. Instead of it staying private, I believe that it started to spread. Amazing how quick we are to spread news that tears people down (I've been guilty of that). Within a week from the news, an email went out congratulating the first intern class for completing the program. My name wasn't listed. Great! Adding more to the speculation. I quickly deleted the email. A co-worker (one who was in the program with me) asked me why my name wasn't in the email. I told him I didn't know. He said maybe it was a mistake. He was going to find out. "No, no need to do that." But, he already left my office. Another co-worker (we were in the program together as well) came by my desk to ask me the same thing. She wasn't happy that my name wasn't listed, and was going to ask leadership what was going on. "No, no need to do that." But, she left my office. I don't want leadership thinking I was asking others to go and speak for me. My head hurts. My heart hurts. Time to get home. I found out that someone else in the class didn't complete the program either. I will check on her tomorrow.

For the next month or two, I was struggling. I wasn't understanding why this was happening to me. Was it because I dated Jason? Why was he coming up? "God is punishing you because you two dated." This couldn't be true. I remember the Singles Pastor saying that God is a forgiving God. Did I ask for forgiveness about dating Jason? I can't remember. "God, I am sorry for dating Jason when I knew he wasn't good for me. Please do not let this be a punishment." I was making sure to continuously attend church, Small Group and the Singles Group. My relationship with some of the ladies began to change. I didn't feel as if I was accepted by some of them. It felt as if they were looking down on me. Like, I was beneath them (where in the Bible are we to do that?). I could tell it was becoming kind of clique-ish. I knew this would happen, so I started to pull back some. "They know." What? Who knows? They know what? About work? "They know." I have to stop listening to this voice. This would take place on the way to work....in the mornings.....where it was quiet. But, whenever I felt tears begin to stream down my face due to the lies that were beginning to sound like the truth, this song would play on the radio..... "I'll praise You in this Storm. And, I will lift my hands." Every time! I also found myself praying and talking to God more driving to and from work. Especially, in the mornings. In the morning.....

I received an email at work that leadership wanted to meet with me. To discuss what happened. I wasn't ready, but this was about to happen. I remember the day of the meeting, I prayed and talked with God. I asked Him to be with me, and for the Holy Spirit to calm the emotions in the room. I remember asking God for His every word to come out of my mouth, and that they saw 'Him' when they looked at me. Time for the meeting. Let me tell you, I wasn't nervous. As I walked over to the meeting, I kept thanking God for being with me. I was ready! As soon as I arrived, the other co-worker who did not complete the program, came storming out of the room. I was shocked. She was so quiet in class. She went storming into the bathroom. I followed behind her. I asked her what was wrong. She was visibly upset. She wanted to start yelling, but I asked her to calm down. She said she thought she could hold it together, but couldn't and started yelling at them. I told her to breathe. I understood she was upset, but we still needed to respect the leaders (where was this coming from). We can't let pride and hurt get in the way. I prayed with her and, told her that she needed to go back to the room, apologize for her outburst, listen to what they had to say, and try to stay calm. She thanked me, and went back to the room. She came out a little better, but I could tell she was still upset. I understood, I was upset myself, but I didn't want them to see that. One of the leaders came out to let me know that they were preparing for me, so to give them about five to ten minutes. Okay, now,

I can tell you something.....I wasn't nervous. Butterflies (the irony) are good for fluttering around in my stomach. Does this happen to you when you are nervous? But, this time, I didn't feel any fluttering. I was at peace. I knew the Holy Spirit was with me, and I had no reason to be afraid. I finally go into the conference room, and sit at the table. There are four in leadership positions at the table. The Head begins with why we are here, and what the outcome will be. He brought up some situations that I was not aware of, which left him perplexed. I never saw a write up of some of what he was mentioning (I was taking notes). He still looked perplexed. He stated that their intent was for me to complete the program three months after the others, but because of a rule that came about, I had to wait a year. Inside, I wanted to die, but that feeling went away quickly. I mean, too quickly. I was put on probation, basically. Like, I could not slip up (I wasn't planning to). After the meeting, I walked back to my office. I will be honest, this was painful, but I had to remind myself that this would go by quickly. And, that God would guide me through this every...step...of...the...way. He would.....right?

Quite a bit was happening in 2011. I was being held back at my job (like, I was in school) with reasons unknown to me. I mean, we had a meeting, but that still didn't explain why I was being held back. The morning drives to work (remember, I lived an hour and half away from my job), were......trying. I say trying because I was still trying to understand why this was happening to me, which in turn, would be me becoming angry about my relationship with Jason. No, I had not heard from him since February, but I was still angry....at myself.....for being in that relationship. So, the lies were coming back. The lies that, once again, were becoming truth. Again, "Why me, God? Why is this happening to me?" *Why not you?* I was beginning to think this was God's favorite saying.......to me. Tears would flow, my song would always come on the radio (remember, 'Praise You in This Storm' by Casting Crowns?), my heart would hurt, my mind was racing.....so much going on. What I was realizing during this time, is that God wanted me to draw closer to Him. An hour and a half to and from work, and the mornings are quieter, so I noticed I was hearing Him more. Isn't this what He wants from us? To spend more time with Him? To hear Him? Now, I wasn't always up for this because I would also hear God tell me to forgive those at work. But, before I get into that, let me explain why the mornings are the best times to spend with God.......ready......because Jesus did it. I know you are probably like, "I thought she was going to be more profound," but that is profound. Let's back it up even more. When you study the Old Testament, even those we read and study about, spent time with God in the morning, and/or moved into their assignment....in the morning. You know the story of Abraham (previously known as Abram) and how God asked him to sacrifice his son, Isaac, the promise? Let's go to Genesis 22. Backstory, Abraham and Sarah (previously known as Sarai) didn't have any children. God promised a child to Abraham and Sarah (no last names, so I can't say, 'Mr. and Mrs. Stevenson'), and they had their 'promise.' Even in their old age, they had a child, and his name was Isaac. Now, Abraham was faithful to God, but he was showing way too much love to Isaac. We serve a jealous God (definitely learning this), and wasn't having that (Danielle's translation). So, in chapter 22, it starts with God testing Abraham. Has God ever tested you? No?! Hmmmm....back to the story. God told Abraham to take his son....his only son whom he loved so much, to the mountains and sacrifice him. Now, hold on! WHAT?! I am not sure about you, but my response would've been like this, "Are you serious, God? You know we've been praying for this child for years. We waited 25 years for this promise. 25 YEARS!!! And, now You want me to sacrifice him?" But, Abraham, being the faithful man of God that he was, obeyed the Lord. Verse 3 reads, **"So Abraham *got up early in the morning*, saddled his donkey, and took with him two of his young men and his son Isaac. He split wood for a burnt offering and set out to go to the place God had told him about."** (Genesis 22:3 Holman Christian Standard Bible (HCSB), *emphasis* added). In the morning. The mornings are typically peaceful, quiet, represents a new day, and our minds are more still.

In the morning......no, God wasn't asking me to sacrifice my child, but He was asking me to still my mind, listen for Him and draw closer to Him. Sacrificing the complaints and choosing to trust in Him. I mean, the drives to work in the mornings were peaceful, but Satan would try to come too. Those lies.....oh, those lies. And, the internal debates within myself......I honestly have no idea how I got to work sometimes. *In the morning*...at times, I didn't like the drive to work. I didn't like to hear God asking me to forgive those at work. He was working on me, and I didn't like it. Do we ever like when God works on us? I am just being honest. I didn't want to forgive what was happening at work. Didn't God know how I was being treated? How I was being looked at? I am sure there is some gossip going around. People who I thought were my friends, started to avoid me. It was like I was a black sheep. If they spoke to me, even said "Hi," they would be black balled. Has this ever happened to you? No one was taking the time to see how I was doing, or how it was affecting me. Didn't God see this? Of course He did. He's God. But, I needed to be the bigger person (I didn't like that). I also felt as if I needed time to do this, plus, the lies kept coming back. The enemy was stirring up the lies about my worth.........that I basically was not worthy. I wasn't worth enough to be in a relationship, and wasn't worthy at work. That everyone at work was talking about me. EVERYONE! No one wanted to work with me, or be around me. That I had no friends. I wasn't pretty enough to stay with Jason. It was my fault we broke up. At times, I had no idea which to listen to. It seemed like the lies were so loud, and would overpower the still voice I was straining to hear. Whose voice am I listening to?

I mentioned that quite a bit was happening in 2011. I began (started back) with purchasing my first home. Now, I tried back in 2010, and I was denied. DENIED!?! What are you talking about?! In 2010, I was trying to be real hardcore against the Lord. Like, who was He to tell me I couldn't get a home?! I truly should not have went there, because God showed me..........real quick. Can I tell you, I was humbled real quick? So, a year has gone by, and I thought to try again, this time, with the guidance of the Lord. I was approved!! Thank You, Jesus!! I remember saying, "God, if this takes six months to a year to get my home, I can do that." Now, deep down, I thought it would be like, two months...three, max. I will never forget Joyce Meyer said that God is a contractual God (I heard her say this at one of her conferences). I didn't know that God would also use this to get me to not only trust Him more, but know that He is the orchestrator. Okay, I must've missed that part, the part where everything in our lives, God would use. Did I fall asleep during that part? So, this process is starting right when I am beginning the....what shall we call it.....the.....the probationary period at my job. No, this isn't too much. This isn't too much at all. Being held back at work, looking for a home, and still fighting these lies that keep popping up. **"We are assured and know that [God being a partner in their labor] all things work together *and*** are [fitting into a plan] for good to *and* for those who love God and are called according to [His] design *and* purpose." **Romans 8:28, Amplified Classic (AMPC).** Whew....this is something.

So, in the process of looking for a home and being held back at work, I wasn't feeling connected with some of the ladies in the Singles Life Group. I would be invited to outings, but I still felt as if I had to prove myself to some of them. Why? Now, I will say that I didn't share with them what was happening at work. Was it judgment that I was afraid of? Is this another lesson? How many can one do at a time? I was beginning to notice the cliques. I was afraid of this. If one of the ladies began dating a gentleman, others would be upset....with her (I am guessing they liked him too). Why be upset with her, if he sought her out? Isn't that what the Bible says, **"He who finds a [true] wife finds a good thing and obtains favor from the Lord. [Proverbs 19:14; 31:10." Proverbs 18:22 AMPC.** But, I guess it's easier to be upset with the young lady. I didn't want to be a part of this. I wanted to learn how to serve God and learn who I am during my season of singleness. So, I found myself not attending some of the events. I was becoming busy with the house hunting, and trying to maintain my sanity at work. Did I mention that I had (still have) trust issues? That would be another reason why I didn't share with these ladies. I didn't feel as if I could trust them. So, I kept a lot inside. Which is not healthy, but, I was used to keeping things inside. Due to fear? Rejection? Hurt? Trust? Where is all of this stemming from?

By summer 2011, I wasn't feeling the urge to attend the Singles Life Group anymore. I would attend church, but not sit with the group (they sat in a particular area). I would try to skip out so that I wouldn't see them. Is this how it's supposed to be at church? Again, did I sleep through something? Have the cliques in church? Be upset at a young woman because the young man sought her out? Jumping in between friends? I wasn't for this. I wanted to grow in my walk with the Lord. A co-worker told me about the church she'd been attending for some years, and said I should join her one Sunday. I know it's not good to just jump from church to church (this is what I was told), but it doesn't hurt to visit another church. Right? I didn't jump right away to visit her church, it was more like a few weeks later. I think I was feeling guilty about visiting another church, but I wanted to learn more about God,

His goodness, my purpose during my season of singleness (however long that may be), and so much more. I didn't want to be distracted by the 'she likes him, but he likes someone else' game. So, I visited my co-worker's church. Right away, I was greeted in the parking lot. Ooookay. He's happy! Then, when I walked up to the building, I was greeted. What's going on? As soon as I got inside the building, I was greeted. Okay, this is......nice, but is this real?! It seemed as if I was greeted with every step I took (basically, that's what happened). I spotted my co-worker in the sanctuary, and sat next to her. The worship was good (I mean, when you sing 'Oceans (Where Feet May Fail)' by Hillsong UNITED, you truly can't go wrong). The sermon was good. I am a note taker, and being that I was still learning so much about Jesus, it was (and still is) important for me to take notes so I could go back and study them later, along with The Bible.

I was enjoying this new church, but I didn't want to move fast and jump into a new church. I had to make sure that it wasn't my flesh (okay, so does this mean that I am growing a bit in my walk with the Lord?). I needed to pray about this. Still house hunting during this time, as well. I truly had no idea how tiresome house hunting could be. When you are a kid, you just pick out your room. When you're an adult...oh my! Location, size, how many bedrooms (two...three....four), how many bathrooms (one...two...), size of the kitchen, garage or no garage (definitely a two car garage), fenced yard, etc...that's a lot. I mean...a lot to deal with. But, I knew it was time for me to purchase a home because I never really had stability. What I mean by that, is I moved so much from a child to a young adult (due to my upbringing). That was basically the way of life for me. I had an apartment while living in Colorado. I was currently living with my mom (yes, that can help to save money), but if I wanted to....how can I say.....build some stability, I needed to actually purchase a house....a home. Now, I was also praying for my husband, but God brought it to my attention that if I am always moving every so often, I would miss my husband. Not that God can't lead him to me, let's remember that God can do anything. But, how could this happen to me if I wasn't.....stable......building a foundation,

"Then Boaz said to his servant who was set over the reapers, 'Whose maiden is this?' And the servant set over the reapers answered,

'She is the Moabitish girl who came back with Naomi from the country of Moab.' And she said, "I pray you, let me glean and gather after the reapers among the sheaves." So she came and has continued from early morning until now, except when she rested a little in the house.' Then Boaz said to Ruth, 'Listen, my daughter, do not go to glean in another field or leave this one, but stay here close by my maidens. Watch which field they reap, and follow them. Have I not charged the young men not to molest you? And when you are thirsty, go to the vessels and drink what the young men have drawn.' Then she fell on her face, bowing to the ground, and said to him, 'Why have I found favor in your eyes that you should notice me, when I am a foreigner?' (This is the part that I need you to focus on....) And Boaz said to her, 'I have been made fully aware of all you have done for your mother-in-law since the death of your husband, and how you have left your father and mother and the land of your birth and have come to a people unknown to you before. The Lord recompense you for what you have done, and a full reward be given you by the Lord, the God of Israel, under Whose wings you have come to take refuge!' **(Ruth 2:5-12 AMP).**

Did you catch that? I know it was a quite a bit, but it's all important. Boaz heard about Ruth. He heard about her character, how she left her home to follow Naomi (her mother-in-law) to a country she knew nothing about, how she was providing for her and her mother-in-law, and how hard of a worker she was. He heard these about her because she was building a foundation, and she was noticed. Did you catch that?! She was noticed.....by the community. This means that others were seeing her character, being able to get to know her, which meant that when her future husband saw her (spoiler alert, you have to read the Book of Ruth), he knew of her. This is what God was showing me. Not that my husband was coming the next day (but, I mean.....), but I needed to be still, and when you are used to moving every so often, that can be hard. But, this was also one of my early assignments from God....house hunting, but allowing Him to pick the location.....everything. Trusting in Him. Okay, I think I can handle this. I think.

Real life struggles taking place now in late summer 2011. Do I stay at my church, or begin to fully attend this new church, and become a member with them? Do I leave my church because I feel as if I am not getting any attention (let's be real, some people do leave because of that)? Do I leave because of the feel of community was no longer apparent as it once appeared? I was truly learning quite a bit from the Pastor at my current church, but was so torn. I had stopped attending the Singles Group and the Bible Study Group. I believe in checking in at times to see how another is doing, especially if I haven't seen that person in a while. This wasn't happening. This is where I felt as if I wasn't getting any attention. Where I felt as if no one cared. So, I found myself attending the new church more and more. The sermons/teachings were really good, and they actually knew my name. I was feeling more welcomed at this church. What do I do, Lord? I do remember my co-worker wanting me to meet someone at this new church, and God was quick to tell me that I was not attending this new church for that. Okay, this means that if I do attend this new church, there's a purpose, and it definitely was not to look for a husband. That is nowhere in The Bible, a woman looking for her husband. Trust me, I've searched all through The Bible, and it's not there. In the Book of Proverbs, in the NLT Version, it states, ***"The man who finds a wife finds a treasure, and he receives favor from the Lord."*** (Proverbs 18:22, *emphasis added*). Did you catch that? He who finds a wife, but his eyes must be on the Lord, first (I added that part). So, no moving to a church to look for a husband, ladies.

By fall 2011, I am still house hunting (how much longer, Lord). I was starting to feel very stressed because I wanted to be in my home. But, that was not the case. I was becoming very impatient, which was leading me to become more frustrated (more that I didn't have my home). But, God is never in a hurry....NEVER. His timing is always perfect....ALWAYS. We have a tendency of trying to hurry up the process, and miss what God is actually wanting to do in and through us (don't worry, I am still learning this). I wasn't enjoying the process. I wanted to hurry this all up, but God (He is something else) was using people to speak to me (God can use anyone and anything....He used a donkey). I remember complaining to a co-worker about not being in my home, and he told me to enjoy the process. He said every home I looked at, use them to help me, or get ideas from those homes. Okay, that made sense. That actually gave me some peace. I made the choice to enjoy the process, not rush it (this was hard), pray and trust in God (this was hard). I began praying that my realtor and I would be on the same page when looking for houses. She was really doing well with the houses, so as if she wasn't far off, but I felt that we could hone in just a bit more. Let me tell you, God answered that prayer real quick. I was beginning to actually enjoy house hunting. Felt like I was on HGTV (you guys watch that station?). Where were the Property Brothers? While still house hunting, I was still dealing with the being held back at work. Looking for a home would take my mind off of the issue, but that was only AFTER work. While at work, I still felt as if I was being judged, talked about, looked down upon....I could go on. And, I began to attend a Bible Study Group with the new church. I was still, kind of, sort of hanging out with some of the ladies from my old church (I hadn't made the 'new' church, my church). I truly cannot explain how I was feeling. Anger, hurt, sadness, excitement, fear, anxiety, loneliness......it was like, all of them.....at the same time. Okay Danielle, what have you been learning at Bible Study? You have to talk with God. He wants to hear from you. But, does He really though?! I mean, He has time to hear from me? The answer is 'Yes.' Like, a resounding 'Yes.' I was talking to God before, but it was still sporadic. Praying a bit more, but still sporadic. I needed to be consistent with spending more time with God. Yes, on the way to work, I was doing that. If a meeting was coming up, or someone was getting on my nerves (let's be real), I would talk to God, but I still wasn't building that relationship with God. A true, genuine and intimate relationship with God. I was believing (again) that God saw me the way others (I was presuming) saw me. Those lies.....they like to pop up when you're down. I can't end 2011 believing the lies. Jesus didn't give up His life for me to listen to the lies. I decided to look up the word 'children' in the Bible, because from my understanding, when I accepted Jesus Christ as my personal Lord and Savior, I became a child of God. The following scripture bursted into my being,

"SEE WHAT [an incredible] quality of love the Father has given (shown, bestowed on) us, that we should [be permitted to] be named *and* called *and* counted the children of God! And so we are! The reason that the world does not know (recognize, acknowledge) us is that it does not know (recognize, acknowledge) Him." – 1 John 3:1 AMP

That scripture brought so much....how can I say it? It brought some awareness about my relationship with God and how He saw me. And, I can call Him, Father? This was new for me. I never really heard anyone call God, Father. He's my Father? Oh wow!!!This revelation took my breath away. But, then, why would my Father allow me to be held back at work? And, feel lonely? Hmmmm.....may need to think about this Father thing.

2012!!! Like, I didn't think it would get here! Okay! New Year! Let's try again. I am no longer attending my church. I was fully engrossed with the Bible Study group at the new church, I mean, I was attending every night (I wouldn't say much, but I always felt that there was something I needed to say). So, my weekdays went like this; up around 4 AM to get ready for work (still living with my mom) to leave by 5:15 AM, to arrive at work around 6:30. God was definitely using that drive time to speak to me, or use a song to speak to me (like I mentioned way earlier). He still wanted me to forgive those at work. No, I am good. I would still ask 'why me,' and God would still say, 'why not you?' I could tell that I was not going to win that conversation, but I still wanted to know why (God never has to explain why. He is Sovereign). I would actually start journaling (again) about my days, and asking God to help me see His purpose and will for me during this season (I am not going to lie, I was afraid of the answer). Get off around 3:00, and head home. Remember, the drive to and from was an hour and a half. Gas, tolls, and traffic (if I didn't get leave from work on time), were wearing me down. How much longer of this, Lord? On the nights there was Bible Study, I would drive to a store in the area, and literally, take a nap in my car. With the getting up early for work and all, I would be so tired. So, nap times in my car until Bible Study started, worked for me.

It had been a couple of years, but I felt like I needed to fast. Yes, I was going to try this again. So, by February (why February, I have no idea), I was fasting. I truly began praying about my home and my job. I wanted to be a light in my neighborhood, in an area God needed me in, and praying it would be close to my job so that I could check on my fur baby during lunch. I did ask for a fenced yard (because of the fur baby) and an actual two car garage. But, also for my home to be a place where women's Bible Studies would take place, as well as Game Nights and other gatherings. I wanted my home to be warm and welcoming to all who would come over. But, it was wherever God wanted me to be for Him. I was definitely making sure to include God in all of this. All still new to me, because I just want to go, or more like, just do it, and then ask God if it's okay, but I was learning that God wanted to be involved in every area of my life. Plus, He is the Captain, so why not let Him lead. He knows the way, which can be scary when our trust is not fully in Him. And, I was still learning to fully put my trust in Him. You may have heard how some people say, "I accepted the Lord, and was fully obedient to Him out of the gate." Really? Because in The Bible, the 12 disciples walked with Jesus every day during His three years in full ministry, and they were not fully obedient to Him. They had doubts, attitudes (Peter was just a spitfire....hot head), they were still selfish, their faith wavered, and you were just all for the Lord just out the gate? I don't believe that. In all honesty, it takes time to fully trust in the Lord. I mean, truly give everything over to Him. I felt the house hunting and being held back at work were just the beginnings of this journey called 'trust.' I will be honest, I wasn't sure how I felt about this, but this is part of our walk with Jesus.

March is here!! Quite a bit was happening. One more month of being on probation at work. This was difficult because I could feel people staring at me, and I am sure they wanted to ask what happened. I still didn't know why I was held back, but my morning drives to work were actually building my prayer life, my time in God's presence and building my trust in Him (look, He was getting me to work while I had tears in my eyes listening to Casting Crowns). I was learning that prayers are conversations with God. There was no fancy way to pray, but have conversations with Him, and......listen (this was hard for me in the very beginning, and still at times now....stubbornness). I had to remind myself that God was for me, and that I wasn't alone. The Apostle Paul (he's a favorite of mine) stated the following:

"What then are we to say about these things? If God is for us, who is against us? He did not even spare his own Son but offered him up for us all. How will he not also with him grant us everything? Who can bring accusation against God's elect? God is the one who justifies. Who is the one who condemns? Christ Jesus is the one who died, but even more, has been raised; he also is at the right hand of God and intercedes for us. Who can separate us from the love of Christ? Can affliction or distress or persecution or famine or nakedness or danger or sword? As it is written: **Because of you we are being put to death all day long; we are counted as sheep to be slaughtered.** No, in all these things we are more than conquerors through him who loved us. For I am persuaded that neither death nor life, nor angels nor rulers, nor things present nor things to come, nor powers, nor height nor depth, nor any other created thing will be able to separate us from the love of God that is in Christ Jesus our Lord." (**Romans 8:31-39**, The Study Bible for Women, Christian Standard Bible (CSB)).

That was quite a bit, but that entire passage was (and still is) a reminder that no matter what we may be going through, God is for us. Satan is the one who condemns, and loves to bring up our past, but not God. God gave up His One and Only Son for us. Jesus was a pleasing sacrifice....painful, but pleasing. He was spared for us so that we could be made whole in and through Him. Jesus did say that we would have trials, "I have told you these things, so that in *Me* you may have [perfect] peace and confidence. In the world you have **tribulation and trials and distress** and **frustration;** but be of good cheer [take courage; be confident, certain, undaunted]! For I have overcome the world. [I have deprived it of power to harm you and have conquered it for you.]" **(John 16:33 AMPC** *emphasis* added). Now, that's in red, so Jesus said this. Notice Jesus said we will have tribulation, trials (felt as if I was going through three at one time), distress and frustration (I was very frustrated), but He tells us to be of good cheer (hold on....what?). Be of good cheer while frustrated and in the midst of a trial? But, Jesus did this all the way to the cross, and on the cross!!! He became fully human, like so human, while dying on the cross that He even asked His Father, Our God, why had He forsaken Him (reference **Psalm 22:1** and **Matthew 27:46**). Jesus was forced into the wilderness after He fasted (forty days by the way), by the Holy Spirit, to be tested. And, we think we're immune to the trials of this world? Even though our Savior told us that we would have trials? We want the blessing part, but not the trial. God was reminding me that it's during the trials, the valleys, the frustrations, the distress is where He wants to mold and refine us. None of us like that (if you do, all the power to you), but these are necessary. Go back to The Book of Exodus, the journey the Israelites took was to be 11 days.....it was a 40 year journey!! 40

YEARS! Why? Because God knew their hearts and how they wanted to cling to the past. The past couldn't come into the Promised Land (I will discuss more of that later). God was leading me into a new area, a new land. Not how I pictured any of this, but, this was also teaching me to trust in Him. Again, not what I was expecting from God, but, Daniel didn't ask to be thrown into the lion's den either, and he made it out with not one scratch on him (read Daniel Chapter 6). Wait....was this my lion's den? Oh, Lord, You will definitely need to guide me through this final month.

By this point, I have decided to become a member of the new church I'd been attending. With all that was going on, I still made sure to attend church every week, be a part of a Bible Study Group, and I was already serving. I felt as if I was growing more in my walk with the Lord, and I was becoming more hungry and thirsty for Jesus. Being that was taking place, why not join? The decision was hard because I truly enjoyed my church. I was learning from the Pastors there, but there were distractions at the church (I know there will be distractions at church, I know). Where I was at the time in my walk the Lord, I felt lead to become a member of the new church. A work (or, works) needed to be done in me, and this was the church that was going to be a part of that. I did have to inform my church about my decision to move on. I was praying for the guidance of the Holy Spirit with writing the letter, and for their response.

So, on top of that, I believe I found a home! How exciting is this. Remember, I'd been praying and seeking God about this. My realtor lead me to an area (I wasn't fond of the area at first sight), but she took me to a more hidden area, you can say. The area seemed pretty quiet (it was during the day and school year). The home was pretty much what I had been praying for; three bedrooms, two baths, an actual two car garage, fenced yard, covered patio, a bonus....skylight in the master bathroom, plenty of space. I liked it right away. After praying and seeking God about it, I put in an offer. Now, I felt so much peace. I wasn't concerned about looking at any more houses. I knew I was lead to my home. I didn't need to stress about it. I didn't share this with anyone. It was between me and God. When He said it was time, I would share with others. God, You have this. He did indeed have this. A few ladies (from my previous church) and I went on a ski trip up in

Gatlinburg, TN. Beautiful place. That Thursday night, I attended Bible Study and was heading out to meet at one of the young ladies' home. I will never forget this conversation. As I was heading out, the owner of the home where Bible Study was held, told me to drive home carefully. I told him that I was heading to a friend's to meet for our ski trip. I remember saying how tired I was driving back and forth, really, the distance, each day. He said this to me, 'God's going to reward for you being obedient in doing that." I was like, I hope sooner than later. He said, "Trust me, God sees it." He told me to be careful and have fun. We left late Thursday night to head to Gatlinburg. We arrived pretty early that Friday morning (we all took turns driving). We checked-in and then when we went to get breakfast (we were starving). While waiting to place our order, I received a phone call. I actually missed the call. It was my realtor. She didn't leave a voice message. I called her back and left her a message. We were able to place our orders. My realtor was calling me back, so I answered the phone:

Realtor: Hey, Dani (I used to go by this name)
Me: Hey, *Sara.
Sara: Dani?
Me: What's up?
Sara: You got the house!
Me: That's great.
Sara: I thought you'd be more excited
Me: I am not alone.
Sara: Okay, let's talk when you have a moment.
Me: Sounds good.
Sara: Congratulations!
Me: Thank you.

I excused myself from the table, went outside, and started crying. Oh my goodness!!! God, is this really happening? I am a homeowner?! I could not believe it. Tears of joy were streaming down my face. I was praising and thanking God! "God, You are doing this for me? I don't deserve this." After gulping some tears, and trying to find my breath, I called my mom. I told her what just happened. I was still crying, so she thought something bad happened, but I told her of what God just did for me. She didn't understand the tears of joy, but it was okay. I was going to continue praise my God. I finally went back inside, still full of excitement and joy. I didn't share with the ladies, because it wasn't time. After the weekend trip, it was time to head back and get started on the whole process of actually getting the home. I had to sign a Good Faith Estimate (GFE) Letter and give $500.00 to say that I wanted the home (not sure if this is done anymore). I had to attend a First-Time Home Buyer's class, which would help put money down for the home. I also had to find an Insurance Company for my mortgage. Okay, this is a lot of work, but these are the steps, and I know God will lead me through. All of this was happening in early April. It was literally, down to the wire when I was able to find an Insurance Company. I learned that when you do not close on your home on the date agreed, the buyer has to pay for the days afterwards (insert eyes emoji here) until the closing. God took care of that. It was time for the closing. This was a big deal for me, so I bought a new dress (I know it's just signing papers, but again, this was a big deal for me). I told one friend about my getting my home, so she was praying for me. The day of the closing, I printed out the HUD-1 Statement, or the Settlement Statement (this shows the breakdown of how the funds are being applied). I contacted the mortgagor and asked how much was I to bring to the closing (I wasn't seeing it on the form). She told me that I wasn't to bring any money, I was actually going to get money back. WHAT???? Money back? Until this day, it cannot be explained in the natural, but I know God had everything to do with that. What I did notice was that my mortgage payment went down about $300.00. OKAY, GOD!! What is happening?! You already know, I was crying in my car (good thing I don't wear eyeliner and mascara). Why, God, are You so good to me? I quickly called my friend and told her the good news. We both began praising God! My mom joined me at the closing, which was a nice surprise. I am actually a homeowner! I could not believe this! April was a good month! I completed the probationary period at my job, and a week later, I closed on my home. I felt that this was a reward for the trial I went through, being held back at my job. It was a pain that God would use and fight for His daughter (I had to get used to saying I was a daughter of God). I will be honest, even after that year, I still didn't know what brought it about. Maybe it was my lion's den. I wasn't touched. I was covered and rewarded. But, as we know, there's never just one trial. Can I say, that my journey with the Lord, was actually just beginning, because it was.

I completed the program and I am in my new home. My dog likes it. He has his own space, and yard. I decided to actually read and study the Bible, from beginning to end. You know how they encourage us to read the Bible in a year, but you read like 6 chapters in a day? Who does that? I cannot do that. I like taking my time reading and taking notes. I have to make sure that I have an understanding of what I am reading, plus I need to apply this to my everyday life. I wanted to read the Bible with 'new eyes.' So, I started in Genesis. Now, when I read **Genesis 5:23-24, "Enoch lived 365 years, walking in close fellowship with God. Then one day he disappeared, because God took him." (NLT)**, I was shook. I am sorry, what happened? God took him? Took him where? Did anybody see this? Did he die? I had questions. I flipped through all of the pages trying to find Enoch. Where did he go? Can he come back? I had to research why God took Enoch (guys, I am not even in Exodus, and I am already trying to save people). This was mind-blowing for me. When I found out that God pretty much protected Enoch from death because he walked so closely with Him, I didn't know how to react. Enoch walked so closely, some versions read 'habitually' with the Lord. You know how breathing is habitual to us, that's how Enoch walked with the Lord. Oh my goodness!!! I want that! Walk so close with the Lord! I was becoming more and more interested....intrigued....with the Bible. After work, I would come home and jump right into the Bible. I was so excited to learn more and more about God, Jesus, the Holy Spirit (so used to hearing him being referred to as the Holy Ghost) and learning that the Holy Spirit is a person, not an 'it.' The Holy Spirit is God's presence and, He dwells within us when we accept Jesus Christ as our personal Lord and Savior.

When we hear someone say, "I had a feeling...", they are referring to the Holy Spirit (if you are walking with the Lord). This was a brand new world opening for me. I was actively attending church, attending Bible Study and serving in the church. I was also meeting more people at my new church, so I was becoming more involved, which was good for me. I am thinking this is it. Starting to get into a comfort zone. Not the case at all.

I didn't mention earlier, but I knew I had the gift of being creative. You ever wonder why you are so good at a particular thing? Like, it seems to just come natural to you? God instills gifts and talents into us well before we are placed in our mother's womb. In the Book of Jeremiah, God told him, **"Before I formed you in the womb I knew [and] approved of you [as My chosen instrument], and before you were born I separated *and* set you apart, consecrating you; [and] I appointed you as a prophet to the nations. [Exodus 33:12; Isaiah 49:1, 5; Romans 8:29.]"** (AMP). Isn't this awesome to know? I will be honest, it still takes my breath away to know that God knows me so intimately. So, you can imagine my surprise, or how shook I was when I first read this. God knows me? Like that? We also know that God is creative. I mean, He created you and me. He created the sky, the butterflies, the rainbow, the trees, the squirrels, the love bugs (not so sure why He created them. And, if you live in the South, then you're familiar with the love bugs. Like, what's their purpose.....), the sunflowers, etc...... But, let's go back to the fact that He created you and me. He didn't speak us into existence, He literally took His time and created us (I am going to dive more into this in a bit. Just wanted to give you a little taste). So, with God being creative, I was creative. Some of us are more creative than others; Chip and Joanna Gaines, The Property Brothers, and Ben and Erin Napier (Home Town) to name a few. I mean, have you seen their shows? You watch them and you're like, "I can totally do that." Then, after about five minutes, you're like, "No, I totally can't do that." That's why they have t.v. shows. I am just over here painting words. But, God was taking that to a different level. I was doing it for peace of mind for me. Now, when I say I was painting words, I would purchase letters from a craft store, pick up some paint and embellishments, and....just....paint. I began painting words like, 'PRAY' because I needed that reminder to pray. DC's Creations had begun a couple of years prior (that's when I thought I would making photo albums and picture frames as a business). God was turning DC's Creations into something else. I remember the peace I would feel as I would paint, with praise and worship music permeating my home (come on, Hillsong UNITED!). Again, I thought I was painting these for me. I would hurry home from work, change into some comfortable clothes, get old newspapers out, have my Bible on the table (I would work in my kitchen), and allow God to show me the colors. Again, He is creative. I will stick to the basic colors pretty fast (you know, blue, red, green, yellow, etc...), but God created colors, so He would show me more. Who would've thought purple and orange went together.

This was new to me. I started placing these words of encouragement around my home and office at work (because I needed it). I looked forward to this time, because I was spending it with God. At times, the Holy Spirit would bring to mind a particular song that contained a particular scripture. I was learning that these songs I was singing along with Casting Crown, Chris Tomlin, Hillsong UNITED, etc. were songs about the Bible. For instance, 'Our God is Greater' by Chris Tomlin (a classic), has this bridge;

"And, if our God is for us, then who could ever stop us?
And if our God is with us, that what can stand against?"

That literally comes from the Book of Romans, chapter 8:31:

"What then shall we say to [all] this? If God is for us, who [can be] against us? [Who can be our foe, if God is on our side?] [Psalm 118:6]" (AMP)

You may have known this, but I had no idea these songs were coming from The Bible. We are literally singing out The Bible. WHOA! This was something for me. I would wonder why certain songs would fill my being. So, working on projects, I think I am starting a business, and allowing God to use this to draw me closer to Him. 2012 was a good year. So many exciting things were happening. Again, now I thought I was good. This would be the way my life would be from this point on. Again.....not the case. Welcome, 2013! How are you? This should be a simple year, right? I mean, I have my home, I am spending more time in The Bible, building up my relationship with the Lord, spending more time with Him, regularly attending church, and Bible Study and still serving. Beginning to hangout a bit more with people from my new church. I think it says somewhere in the Bible that if you no longer attend a church, you no longer communicate with one another. I am pretty sure it says that in.......hold on.........let me find it real quick.......no, it doesn't say that at all. There were a few ladies I thought I would still be able to stay in touch with, but that was not the case. My feelings weren't hurt, I think I was more disappointed. But, God had new people for me to meet and build friendships with. Speaking of friendships, this is about the time I met a woman who would play a BIG part in my walk with the Lord. Her name was *Paula. We said 'Hi' to each other a few times in the hallway, but God, knowing that His daughter (me) loves to eat, had Paula and I actually have our first conversation due to food. She makes the best pound cake (insert the emoji hand claps behind each word)! HANDS DOWN! She made one for someone (by request), but that person was not there. Paula asked if I wanted it, and of course, I was not going to turn it down. That pound cake was so good (I wonder if she can make me one now)! I devoured it in less than 10 minutes. This is how our relationship started. I would find myself in her office a lot, like...a lot. She had so much wisdom about walking with the Lord, I wanted to soak it all in. Like, I wanted to spend days in her office, just to hear what she had to say about how good God is, and why He sent His Son, Jesus and the purpose of staying in the Word, the importance of prayer, and so much more. I had no idea God placed this woman in my life for the season I was in. I would share with Paula the different things God was doing in my life, and how I wanted to be married, and wondering about my purpose, etc.... She would just look at me with a little smile, and would just.....listen. I never really had that before. Someone to just listen to me, not critique or speak over me, was new to me. I could learn a lot from this strong woman of God. She would drop little nuggets of wisdom, and I would soak it all in. I felt like I had my own personal Joyce Meyer. Now, she would say something that would hit me at times (okay a lot of times), but I needed it. Okay, so more growing to take place in my walk with the Lord. 2013 was all about more growing, and having a strong woman of God walk with me during this season. You already know what I'm thinking.......this is good. Life is good. I am good. I am staying diligent in attending church, and being more active. This is it, right God? *No, my child, not even close.*

Whew! Can you believe 2014 is here?! I know you are probably like, "She's going to hit every year?" Maybe. God was working in this one. Whenever I thought I was good, God would come with something else. That's how He works. With that said, there was a stirring in my being. I would remember mentioning this to Paula at times. I wanted to know my purpose, the plans God had for me. In **Jeremiah 29:11**, the Lord said, **"For I know the plans I have for you," says the LORD. "They are plans for good and not for disaster, to give you a future and a hope.""** (NLT). We quote that one pretty well. Paula taught me something that has stuck with me up to this very moment. She taught me to read beyond the well quoted verses. One or two before, and after. Well, we love to quote **Jeremiah 29:11**, but have you read and studied the following verses after? Let's do that:

"In those days *when you pray, I will listen. If you look for me wholeheartedly, you will find me.* I will be found by you," says the LORD. "I will end your captivity and restore your fortunes. I will gather you out of the nations where I sent you and will bring you home again to your own land."" **(Jeremiah 29:12-14, NLT**, *emphasis* added).

God was speaking through the prophet Jeremiah to the Israelites. The Israelites in the Bible were very stubborn and disobedient, much like we are today. God wants our hearts, our full hearts, but He is a gentleman, so He will not force us. We always want the blessings, but not do what God asks of us (trust me, I am still working on the stubbornness part). When we pray, God listens. Do we honestly look for Him wholeheartedly? I mean, with our entire hearts? When we do, we'll find Him. God is never far from us....EVER!!! He is always with us, but do we look for Him with our entire hearts? When we do look for Him with our entire hearts, we find Him...we find the plans He has for us. This is what was happening to me. I wanted more of God, more of His heart, which meant I needed to search for Him with my entire heart. God started revealing to me His heart for women. How much He loves women and the important roles they play in His Kingdom. Okay, now God, You are asking someone who never really had a lot of girlfriends because of the pettiness that takes place.....oh you know. So, why choose me for this? Again, God will use anyone...ANYONE to fulfill His plans. Remember earlier when I mentioned that I had a mouth (still do)? God was going to use this mouth. What we also have to realize is that God will call us for such an assignment, because it's something that we need as well. Did you hear me? WE NEED AS WELL. I needed to learn how to have better relationships with women (something that truly just hit me), and myself. What better way to do this than to give someone, like me, a ministry about women knowing their worth in Jesus and being there for each other. A Sisterhood, if you will. Really, Lord? Okay, if You say so. I really thought this still fell in line with the painting, so I started painting words of encouragements for some of the women at my job. 'PRAY' and "FAITH' were the words that kept coming to my heart. I would ask their favorite colors, and then surprise them with these words.

Paula was a true advocate with this. She would purchase a word from me, and have it in her office for others to see. Then, I started painting 'Prayer Boxes.' Paula was the one who told me that I should start selling these. Like, make money from this? Surprisingly, a few women did place orders for a prayer box. One even told me the price I was charging was too little, with all of the work I put into making the boxes. She said she could see them being sold in stores. Oh really?! This was encouraging to me. So, I literally started a price list. I tried creating a website (not my forte. I know how to go to a website, and click where I need to be). I had cards made, 'DC's Creations.' The initials stood for my name. This is what You wanted me to do, Lord? I can do this. I enjoyed painting.....it was like therapy for me. It would be me, the Lord, praise and worship music, the Bible.....and my little fur baby wanting attention. I would find myself painting at all hours of the night, until the wee hours of the morning, like, right up until it was time for me to get up and get ready for work. But, I lived near my job, so I wasn't too concerned. Just as long as I was able to stay alert at work, and of the schemes of the enemy (he likes to get you when you are weak and not alert). Wow, Lord!!! 2014 is about to be an amazing year!! Business on the horizon, okay. I remember Paula telling me that I would be a speaker, and that I had a lot to say. Okay, I don't think the world is ready for that. For this mouth.....no, not ready. But, she would say it often. Can I be honest, I absolutely believed her. I believed her because I was starting to feel a stirring in me to do that. But, I didn't think I qualified to do that. Who would listen to me? I am not Joyce Meyer. I used to think Paula told me this because I was always in her office.....ALWAYS, sharing what was on my heart and what God was doing in and through me. I am sure she wanted to just work, but it never showed on her face or demeanor, that's another reason why I enjoyed spending time with her. She made time for me. Reminds of me reading and studying about Jesus in the Bible. He always made time for the brokenhearted, the hurting, and the outcasts. He didn't shun anyone away from Him, even if it was just to be healed by Him, and He made the time. Even on His way to spend time with His Father, if someone pressed to get to Him, He made the time for that person and His Father. Paula reminded me of that. Okay, so I am painting and I am going to be speaking in front of people? I am ready! Let's do this! *Not so fast, Danielle. Still have some work to be done in you.*

REFLECTION

As you read in chapter 7, I was going through quite a bit. When our journey starts with the Lord, it's never....simple. I was still new to my faith, so doubts were naturally flooding my mind (take every thought captive, **2 Corinthians 10:5**). We also know that Satan does not stop telling his lies the more we walk with the Lord. What lies are Satan **still** telling you? And, what scriptures are you meditating on to refute those lies?

CHAPTER 8
GLORIFYING GOD
IN MY PAIN

Forgiveness is a Choice

"Be gentle *and* forbearing with one another and, if one has a difference (a grievance or complaint) against another, readily pardoning each other; even as the Lord has [freely] forgiven you, so must you also [forgive]." (Colossians 3:13 AMP)

"For if you forgive others their offenses, your heavenly Father will forgive you as well. But if you don't forgive others, your Father will not forgive your offenses." (Matthew 6:14-15 CSB)

"Then Peter came to him and asked, "Lord, how often should I forgive someone who sins against me? Seven times?" "No, not seven times," Jesus replied, "but seventy times seven!" (Matthew 18:21-22 NLT)

So, 2014 was ramping up to be a busy year, more like being productive. Yes, I was still attending church every week. I made sure to attend Bible Study every week, and still serving. Now, I do not know about you, but I can be the type of person where God says, *"This is going to happen."* I am like, let's do this now. Like, I want to see movement happening......ASAP! But, we know this is not how God works. There's a process. There's always a process. We don't like the process, we want to get to the results....like, two months ago. Not you? This is just me? Okay, I have no problem sharing this part of my journey because it's ongoing. Well, remember when I told you that Paula kept reminding me that I had a lot to say, a change began to take place. More...like...a...shift. I felt God telling me that I would be a speaker and go out and share the Word. I was like, "OKAY GOD!!! I definitely can do that! Go out and share The Gospel, so for it! Put me in, Coach!" Now, how this was coming about may seem strange to you, but it will actually make sense throughout this chapter. I was beginning to notice that whenever I read a story, saw a movie, heard on the news or even during our Sexual Harassment trainings at work, I would feel a righteous anger rise up in me. There was a training video playing, and it was pertaining to rape. Again, an anger was rising up in me. I didn't know why. Then I heard God say, *"Satan is attacking women."* "I know God. What am I supposed to do?" This continued into 2015.

2015 was here, and DC's Creations was not really budging. Did I make this up? I thought I was going to have a ministry for women? I thought I was going to be out and about speaking at seminars and conferences. What's happening? Remember the stubbornness of the Israelites I talked about earlier? I was becoming like them. You see, in Bible Study, I would always feel the Holy Spirit nudge me to say something, but I would downplay it (I still kind of do, but I am definitely getting better at responding). I remember one night at Bible Study, the pastor asked if anyone had anything to say. Everyone was quiet. One of the young ladies, looked over at me, and said, "Dani, do you have something to say?" First off, I didn't like being put on the spot. She just called me out like that. Second.....no, it was just the first off. I responded with a 'no.' After Bible Study, the young lady said this to me, "Dani, God wants to do so much through you. It's so exciting! You have so much to say. You just have to let Him have access." Now, I thought I was giving God access, but then like I mentioned before, stubbornness. And, I can't say that I didn't know I was being stubborn, because I know that I am, but I truly thought I was giving God access. But, when the Lord tells us to say something, and we don't, that's being disobedient. I was being disobedient. So, I needed to be called out. I got offended because it was true. I did have something to say, but I was afraid to say it.....because....what if.....what if I didn't receive any of the, "ooooohhhhhh! That's good!" Let's be real, some of us thrive off of those. But, what if I didn't get at least one, and I only got crickets...or, the dead stare? I would've felt that I didn't say I what I had to say correctly. So, I didn't say anything. Again, this is disobedience to the Lord, and stubbornness is a form of rebellion (Yes, you heard me correctly. It is a form of rebellion). This was something God definitely had to work on me, if I allowed Him to. And, I wanted Him to, but I somehow still wanted it my way. Oh, did I also mention that my Life Group Leader was preparing me to be a Life Group Leader?! ME!!! Well, I was stubborn about that, and still wanted to do it my way. Oh, Danielle. You have so much growing to do. Why are you afraid to let God fully in? Why does it have to be your way? What pain are you holding onto? The pain....makes...me... feel...safe...

You read that I was being prepped to be a Life Group Leader. Again....me to be a leader? Remember some pages back where I discussed that God has given all of us gifts and talents that will help further His Kingdom......well, being a leader is a gift that God gave me. I fought it back then, and I still kind of do now (just being honest). In my mind, who would listen to me (remember, I am also to go out and speak to women about their worth in Jesus)? Do you know anyone like that in The Bible? No? Yes? The one reluctant leader that stands out to everyone is our man, Moses. Good 'ole Moses. You've heard of him, right? We actually meet Moses in the Book of Exodus (Chapter 2, to be exact), but he wrote the first five books of The Bible, which are called 'The Pentateuch' (Genesis, Exodus, Leviticus, Numbers and Deuteronomy). You can read about Moses's birth in Chapter 2, as well as his escape to Midian. It's in Chapter 3 where Moses has his encounter with God. You've heard about Moses and the Burning Bush? It's in Chapter 3. Okay, here we go (so exciting). The angel of the LORD appears to Moses in a form as a blazing fire in the middle of a bush. Moses stared at the bush in amazement (can't say that I would have done the same). The bush did not burn up, even though it was engulfed in flames (again, I don't think I would have been staring at the bush). Here we go:

"When the LORD saw Moses coming to take a closer look, God called to him from the middle of the bus, "Moses! Moses!" "Here I am! Moses replied. "Do not come any closer," the LORD warned. "Take off your sandals, for you are standing on holy ground. I am the God of your father – the God of Abraham, the God of Isaac, and the God of Jacob." When Moses heard this, he covered his face because he was afraid to look at God." **(Exodus 3:4-6, NLT).**

Now, I am going to stop here for a moment. Okay, so God called out to Moses from the middle of the bush. Again, I would have not stayed around the burning bush (I was taught to not hang around fires), but God saw that Moses was intrigued, curious and amazed. Did you notice how God got Moses's attention? Through the burning bush. God knew that would get this man's attention. What has God used to get your attention? Back to Moses. Now, Moses responded when God called him (I did the same in 2012). Did you notice that God called him by his name? God knows each of us by our names (this is just so exciting to me). What I like about the mentioned verses, is how God told Moses Who He was. He didn't come out saying, "BOOM!! I am God! You better recognize!" No, God stated Who He was with a comfort to Moses. God is the God of his forefather(s), Abraham, Isaac and Jacob. Moses could relate to that. He could relate that The One

Who created the world is the God of his forefathers. When God called me to serve Him, he got me at the end of my yoga class. I was already at peace and rest, and His still, small voice came in. I wasn't frightened. I was actually, intrigued, curious, that this small voice was calling out to me. I had nothing to be fearful of. Moses covered his face, I covered mine (I had that little towel to go over my eyes). Now, I couldn't see God, but I heard Him. I knew He was there in that yoga room with me. Moses covered his face because He was afraid to look at God, I am going to say, I would have done the same thing. I am a mess, how could I look at God. I am thinking Moses felt the same, and because, this is the God he's heard about. Let's keep going.

"The LORD told him, "I have certainly seen the oppression of my people in Egypt. I have heard their cries of distress because of their harsh slave drivers. Yes, I am aware of their suffering. So I have come down to rescue them from the power of the Egyptians and lead them out of Egypt into their own fertile and spacious land. It is a land flowing with milk and honey – the land where the Canaanites, Hitties, Amorites, Perizzites, Hivites, and Jebusites now live. Look! The cry of the people of Israel has reached me, and I have seen how harshly the Egyptians abuse them. Now go, for I am sending *you* to Pharaoh. *You* must lead my people Israel of out Egypt." **(Exodus 3:7-10, NLT** *emphasis added).*

"Okay, hold on God!!! What's happening? You want me to do what? Like, I know Who You are and all, but You want me to do what? I must lead the people out of Egypt? What's happening, again?" I am picturing this is what Moses is thinking. I mean, I am thinking this for him. Remember when I told you that God spoke to me and said, *"Satan is attacking women."* I knew this, but what was I to do? Little ole' me?

"But Moses *protested* to God, "Who am I to appear before Pharaoh? *Who am I to lead* the people of Israel out of Egypt?" **(Exodus 3:11, NLT** *emphasis added).*

Let's talk about this for a moment, or......forever. Moses protested to God. We can protest due to righteous anger, for example, injustice towards others due to race, gender, sexual assault, religion, to name a few. But, to protest to God, that is rebellion. Why do we protest to

God? Because we are fearful of the call He's placed on our lives (from the beginning, mind you). We think we need to be super qualified, so well educated in that particular area, and that we are alone in that call. All of this is not true. But, I felt Moses. "Who am I to...?" Don't we do this often with God? Let me be clear, I did this often with God (still kind of do). "Who am I to do anything to help women being attacked by Satan? Who am I to go and speak about this stuff, about The Bible?" Yet, I knew that I was to be a speaker and, I knew that I was a leader, I just didn't want the leading part. Just let me speak. But, the two would need to go hand-in-hand for what God had called me to do. But, I was still protesting this leader thing. "Who am I?" Moses, my man, I feel you. Let's see what God has to say.

"God answered, "I will be with you. And this is your sign that I am the one who has sent you: When you have brought the people out of Egypt, you will worship God at this very mountain." (**Exodus 3:12**, NLT).

Okay, so we know that God is always with us (I mean we should know this). And, God does give signs. He spoke through Paula to get to me about speaking. First, Paula was strong, God-fearing and could hear God like we hear birds chirping. She was so attuned to the Holy Spirit, I was about jealous of that. I wanted that! She kept telling me that I had a lot to say. Then, in Life Group, one of the young ladies told me (called me out, let's be real) that I had so much to say, and how God wanted to use me. But, about that stubbornness.....yeah, that good 'ole stubbornness. She did not want to leave. Stubbornness wanted to stay like, "Girl, I am here for you. We are friends until the end. The very end." *"Let go of the stubbornness."* God wasn't going to send Moses to Pharaoh without guidance and a plan. That's not God. When God calls us to an assignment, we are not going in blind, although that's how it feels. And, we wonder, again, how are we qualified for the call? We want all kinds of signs (I mean, I do) that we are actually on the right path. We want 'certain' people to validate us (even though God did that when He called us), and we want to make sure that there are no bumps in the roads (just smooth sailing, Lord). We don't want to be alone, and we forget that God is with us. We become fearful, and want to *protest* to God. If you are like me, I prefer step by step guidance from the Lord. I mean, if He's going to call me for such an assignment, give me steps. Like, what's going to happen at each moment. So, I am speaker who is to go out and somehow help women who've been attacked by Satan......does God know who I am? The answer is 'yes.' A resounding, 'Yes!' Remember in Jeremiah? God knew you before He placed you in your mother's womb. But, we seem to forget that. What was Moses's response.....protest?

"But Moses *protested*, "If I go to the people of Israel and tell them, 'The God of your ancestors has sent me to you,' they will ask me, 'What is his name?' Then what should I tell them?" God replied to Moses, **"I AM WHO I AM.** Say this to the people of Israel: **I AM** has sent me to you." (**Exodus 3:13-14, NLT** *emphasis* **added**).

Look, I am feeling Moses. He continues to protest to God in Chapter 4 to the point where God became angry with Moses. We'll discuss more of that in a bit. But, I understood Moses's plight. "What do I say when someone asks me, 'Who are you to go out and speak to women? Who said you're a speaker?'" This is where I would stay quiet, and not say what the Holy Spirit was leading me to say. As for the leadership? I mean, I was an Assistant Manager at a national rental car company. But, so were so many others. And, I was serving at church, begrudgingly I might add. Setup was on Saturday evenings, and then serve all day on Sundays. I believe I purposefully had attitude during this time. Little did I know, that God would use this time to push me into that leadership position that I was *protesting* about. Even while serving, I had people tell me that I would make a great leader. I would snort at this, because......why? I remember one Sunday, a few ladies just 'randomly' kept asking me, "What if they ask you today to be a lead (I was serving in Hospitality)?" I was like, "I will say 'no.' This mouth and attitude? They don't want this." Well, they sure did ask me to be a lead (did my attitude not reflect that I didn't want to do that? I thought I was strong with that attitude?). I, begrudgingly (very), said 'yes.' Why me? See, this attitude and disposition were not of the Lord, but God wasn't done with me (thank You, Jesus). We have to start somewhere, right? It could've been while I was working at the rental car company, but that wasn't the place. A new chapter of my life had started, and this is where God tapped me on the shoulder. I just needed to allow God to do what He needed to do, and stop fighting Him. Sounded easy, right? Remember when I said that I was being prepped to be a Life Group Leader? Definitely fought that. I stopped attending that Bible Study Group because.....of.....what? I was going to have a Women's Only Life Group. This was going to teach me how to walk the steps God laid out for me. Teach me how to tone in with my words, and build relationships with women (young and old). Nope! I wanted to do it my way, because I knew the way, right? Let me hold my own Bible Study (it went from like 20 women to 4 by the time it ended. My pride was very apparent). I was going to try to make this happen in my way. No, Danielle. It's God's way, or the hard way. For some reason, I was choosing the hard way. Why is that? Sounds like I was choosing the way of the Israelites.

As 2015 was churning, I was still fighting this leadership thing. Even at work. Okay, God. You're getting me here too? My goodness! Let me tell you, fighting was not (still is not) the word. I was so defiant about not stepping into a leadership role at work. Why? The reason, like the honest reason, I was still hurt from what happened to me a few years prior. I was hurt, angry, bitter and resentful. At the time, I didn't realize this, but it was obvious. Why would I want to be a leader? Plus, I was in my feelings about how slow my business was moving. I wanted to see movement....ASAP!! I can be honest with you, right? I was expecting my business to be flourishing by this time. I was expecting women and men to order words of encouragement, as well, as prayer boxes. I thought I would be painting every night and the weekends. This wasn't happening. I wasn't getting it. What all do I need to do? You know those baby steps I was speaking about earlier, I completely wanted to bypass all of that, and just move into the BIG part. I wanted to walk into my 'Promised Land,' but without the training. Again, not the way of the Lord. And, on top of that, I wanted to be married. What's the deal?! Any single ladies out there feel my plight? Now, I would be in Paula's office lamenting all of this to her. Again, she would have a little smirk on her face (it was like God was looking at me saying, *"Oh, daughter. If you only knew all of the goodness I have in store for you. Just be patient, and trust in Me."*), take notes (more like, what God was telling her), and listen. That part always got me. She would let me spill it all out, and wouldn't make me feel less than. One day I did all of this, and she just looked at me. I could tell that the Holy Spirit was talking to her. I asked her what did He say. She was almost hesitant, but finally said, "Have you forgiven your uncle?" What?! That stopped me in my tracks. I looked at her for a moment, then excused myself from her office, and went back to mine. Where did that come from, Lord? That pondered in me for the rest of the day, until I got home. Remember the movie, 'War Room?' After that movie, I immediately turned my closest into my prayer/war room, and that is exactly where I went as soon as I got home. I remember asking God, "Didn't I forgive my uncle, Lord?" There was an altercation some years back, and I held bitterness against him for years. If he came around, I would go into another room. That's how bad it was. As time went on, I thought I had forgiven him, but what I really did was just suppress and cover it. This took me by surprise! I immediately asked the Lord to help me forgive my uncle. You see, when we don't forgive those that have offended us, we are never really free. What we do is just sweep the issue under the rug, and hope over time that it goes away....and never return. But, until we face it, or acknowledge the offense, it will just keep coming back. I didn't want this offense to hang over me for the rest of my life. I wanted to be free. "Lord, help me to forgive my uncle for the offense that was committed against me. I ask You to touch his heart. You do not condemn, but you do convict. May we not continue to point fingers, but allow You to do a work in each of us. May pride and rebellion be removed from us, and in their place, the grace and mercy that You so kindly extend to each of us. Help me, Lord to see my uncle the way You do, not how Satan wants me to see him. May I no longer carry any bitterness, anger and resentment in my heart towards him. And, if I have offended him in anyway, please reveal this to me so that, I too, can be free. In Jesus's Name. Amen." That was my prayer. I cried a bit, but I felt.....free.....like a weight had been lifted off of my shoulders. I stayed in my prayer closest a bit longer, to continue to stay in God's Presence. So peaceful. The next day, I went into Paula's office and thanked her for bringing that to my attention. She told me she was hesitant to say anything, because she didn't know how I would respond, but the Holy Spirit kept pressing her to say something. She said, "I have to be obedient to what the Lord tells me." I so wanted to get to that level, I just needed to stop trying to be in control, stop being stubborn and stop being prideful. Work in progress.

God was about to get me in another area. When I got saved in 2009 at Joyce's conference, I started to feel God wanting to do so much in me, but, as you can read (see), I was *protesting* to Him. I would notice, at times, whenever I would pray I would feel.....a sensation.....fall upon me. And, I knew what it was, but, you already know, I fought it. I was fighting the gift of being able to speak in tongues (bear with me, this all lines up). The reason? I wanted to be in control when I prayed. I wanted to know what I was saying. Now, remember when God told Moses that He would give him a sign? God was giving me signs that I was to have this gift. Again, I played it down, and was more like, "Why would I have that gift?" Yet, I wanted the gift. Come on, Danielle. Aren't you tired of trying to do things your way? I would be in awe when listening to others speak in tongues, but I was afraid to have it. A woman I met at a Hillsong Worship concert brought this to my attention. We kept in touch after the concert, and decided to meet up for lunch one day. I mentioned how God kept wanting me to speak in tongues, but I was afraid to release it to Him. She said she wanted to ask me at the concert if I could speak in tongues, but waited. So, at the beach, she started to pray and ask God to loosen my tongue and my let down my guard, so that I would be able to speak in the Heavenly language that was ordained for me. Now, we were on the beach, so I was well aware of people walking by. I was concerned about what they were thinking in seeing us on the beach asking for the Lord to loosen my tongue. The woman told me what I already knew. She said that the gift was in me, I just needed to loosen up, and not want to be in control. She told me to pray about it because it was a gift God wanted to give me. So, I prayed about it. I literally went into my prayer/war room, and lifted up a heartfelt prayer to God about being able to speak in tongues. Now, this was to be my own Heavenly language between God and me. This was not to interpret in front of others. There is a gift of interpreting tongues that is to edify the church. Have you read the book, 'Praying For Your Elephant: Boldly Approaching Jesus with Radical and Audacious Prayer' by Adam Stadtmiller? If not, you need to. The overall of the book is to teach us to pray very specifically and very detailed. God is very detailed. You don't believe me? Read about when God told Noah to build the ark for the flood (Genesis 6), The building of The Tabernacle (Exodus 25-27), and how about one more......you. Let's go to Genesis for a moment,

"Then God said, "Let us make man *in our image, in our likeness,* and let them rule over the fish of the sea and the birds of the air, over the livestock, over all the earth, and over all the creatures that move along the ground." So *God created man in his own image, in the image of God he created him; male and female he created them.*"(**Genesis 1:26-27**, New International Version (NIV) *emphasis* added).

Did you catch that? God made you and me in His image. He didn't rush it (just read how He made Adam (**Genesis 2:7**). Your hair (curly, straight, the color), eye color, nose (whether you like it or not), freckles (if you have them....they are so beautiful), shape of your mouth, your laugh, and more. So, when I prayed about speaking in tongues, I was very specific. I'll share the prayer with you (I wrote it out on October 25, 2015:

Prayer: Holy Spirit, I desire to speak in tongues. I know that the ability is in me. Please reveal to me why am I suppressing the blessing/gift? What am I truly afraid of? I know and believe that being able to speak in tongues will heighten my gifts that have been given to me by you. I desire to be obedient in all things. Please help loosen my tongue! I want to be open, and receive they flame of the Holy Spirit!

That was my prayer! At the bottom of the paper, I wrote: Turn on the flames of the spiritual gifts that have been given to me! I was very serious about getting this gift. 40 days later, the gift came!!! My tongue was loosed, and it seemed like everything that was bottled up just came out. My pastor reminded me to continue praying and speaking in tongues my first year. He said a lot of Christians lose it because they feel as if they are not speaking in tongues, so they lose the gift (the works of the enemy). I will tell you, I pray and speak in tongues as much as I can. No longer fearful of it because I know the power behind it.

Now, we are in 2016! I am still fighting being a Bible Study Leader, not seeing movement with DC's Creations, still a lead in Hospitality at church, questioning my purpose and waiting for the husband (just being real). I could tell a change was taking place, I just didn't know what it was. With DC's Creations, I was now painting canvases. Okay, Lord. I am painting words of encouragement, prayer boxes and canvases. Will anyone be buying these? I had the wrong mentality. On the surface, I was thinking this was for women, but deep down, I also wanted to make some money. I was dishing out money to make these items, but hardly getting any sales. And, the ones that did purchase from me, were my friends. I should've been more appreciative of them purchasing from me, but that flesh......man, that flesh. It's weak!!! Ahhhh!!!! Oh, and I am still not trying to be in a leadership position at work. Right when I was about to give up on DC's Creations, one of my friends, *James, came into the picture. James and I have been friends since we started working for the organization back in 2008. We kept in touch over the years, but God had our paths cross for a purpose. James knew about DC's Creations (he ordered a few things from me), and he believed in its purpose. I explained I wanted to give up on it because I wasn't seeing any movement with it, and I was doubting if this was really from God (SN: when God gives us an assignment, it's not easy. Remember, the trials and tribulations.....). He asked if I created a website for DC's Creations, and I explained that I tried to, but got discouraged (again, creating a website, not my thing. To go to a website, and click on the items I want to purchase or read, I'm here for it). He said he knew someone that could help with creating a website. Oh really?! Thank You, God! He got us in touch, and I had a meeting with the young woman. The young woman absolutely loved the message behind DC's Creations, and some of the artwork I presented to her. This is awesome! We starting discussing the layout I was looking for on my website; showcase the artwork, a tab for women to submit their prayer requests (I like praying for others), order forms, a tab for me to able to put up devotionals each day, a tab for women lifting encouragements to one another, and so much more. She told me she could create a website like that, and that it would take time (of course). She gave me a quote for the website. It seemed doable. I was so excited! I couldn't wait to tell James. The next day, I shared with him how the meeting went. I told him the cost of the website, and right away, he told me he would pay for website. Hold on.....WHAT?! I didn't know what to say. James told me he could see how big this ministry would be and believed in the purpose, so he wanted to help. OH....MY.....GOODNESS!!! I wasn't expecting this, but remember what God told Moses, that He would give Him a sign. God was definitely giving me signs, I just needed to stay constantly aware of His signs.

So, DC's Creations seems to be back on track, I am still trying to *protest* about being a Life Group Leader (like, just let it happen, Danielle), I am still a lead in Hospitality at church, still a little bitter about what happened at work, so some rebellion was still there (*protesting* about putting in for leadership spots), I was running half marathons (three years in) and guess what...fasting again. Now, I am not sure how this came about, but a co-worker was telling me how her and a few friends were going to do a group fast. I thought that was cool. That was the end for me....or, so I thought. I told her I would think about it. One day, she sent me a text asking for my address. I knew we were supposed to hangout later that weekend, so I sent it to her. God is no joke! Within two days, I had a package from Amazon. I didn't order anything from Amazon, but the package had my name on it. I was like, "God, what is this?" He said to open the box. Inside were two books; 'The Daniel Fast' by Susan Gregory and 'Fasting Journal' by Jentezen Franklin. I knew exactly who sent them to me. I sent a text to my co-worker, and thanked her for being obedient to God and sending the books to me. I guess I am fasting.....again. This took place in June of 2016. I wrote down my reasonings for fasting during this time:

- For direction (clear) about my life and how to move into my calling
- Removal of lust because the stronghold can no longer overtake me.
- Obedience to my Heavenly Father
- My relationship with my family

What was I fasting from:

- Meats
- Sweets
- Social Media
- Pasta
- Wine
- Alcohol

I wrote the following in my journal pertaining to my own personal reason for fasting:

"I know that I have been feeling disconnected from the Lord because I was trying to do things my way and when I wanted. I was being rebellious. I deeply desire to have my connection with my

Heavenly Father. Walk in His ways. I want what grieves the Lord to grieve me."

That was my heartfelt reason, and it still brings tears to my eyes now. I was so desperate for God! Have you ever been there? So desperate for God, that it made you weak? That was me. God knew I needed to fast, and I was going to take this very seriously. As I read through the journal (yes, I still have it), I am seeing reminders of wanting to be obedient to Him, stay in the Word, stay filled in the Spirit, for my eyes to be open in the spiritual, to stay alert of the schemes of the enemy, to increase the anointing that God has given me for the ministry, and more. The three things God showed me during my fast:

- Leadership (church and work)
- The women's ministry He's given me
- My husband

Oh wow!! Let me tell you, that fast was probably the most humbling one that I had done up to that point. Remember, God gives signs about what He's called you to do. He'll show you the 'Promised Land,' but won't show the steps to get there. That's where He does the work. You know, the work we don't like. We want the mountaintops, but it's in the valleys where God does the work that is needed on us. And, we can be in the valleys for as long God needs us to be in the valley. Come on, the journey the Israelites took from Egypt to Mount Sinai to Kadesh- barnea, should've been 11 days....it took 40 years. 40 YEARS!!!!!!!!!!!!!!!!!!!!!!!!!!!! Why? This was due to their sin, rebellion, pride, selfishness, complaining and more. 11 days......40 years! Now, I don't want to spend 40 years in the wilderness. Just to be out there, wandering around and not listening to the One Who knows absolutely best because He's been here before. See, it's easy to say that and fuss at the Israelites, "How could they behave that way? Didn't trust in Him when he parted the Red Sea? When God fed them manna from the sky? When He was their source of light, day and night?" See, we can say that, but we do the same thing. We are good when we see the 'sign,' but then we fall right back into complaining. Right back into doubt. Right back into selfishness. Right back into.......us. We find it easier to complain, than to be thankful for what God is doing and where He is taking us. We fall into complacency.....being lazy....and....comfortable. We prefer our past, and look back at it like it's comfort.....like it's.....a safety net (remember Lot's wife). I didn't want that. So, another sign came my way....

There was a woman I met in Walmart, back in 2014. What connected us? She had a dog (first and foremost) and he looked like my dog. Let me tell you, if I see a dog and its owner, most of the time, I am going to love on that dog, then say 'hi' to the owner, and back to loving on the dog. That's pretty much what happened here, but there was something about the woman that had me focus on her. Her, her husband and I talked for like an hour. I just ran my first 5k that morning, so I wasn't looking all dapper, but we had a great conversation. We talked about God, Joyce Meyer (my spiritual mom, she just doesn't know it), our dogs and our journey. We said we should see Joyce together the next time she came to Orlando (Joyce typically came to Florida every year, alternating between Orlando and Tampa....and I was always there). We exchanged numbers and kept in touch, via text. Well, Joyce did come back to Orlando in 2015, and I was there. I actually volunteered that year. It was awesome!! I was helping out at Israel Houghton's table, when I heard someone say, "Danielle?" I looked around, and saw the lady I met at Walmart the year prior! How she knew where I was, only God. We talked for a moment, and said we had to meet up for lunch. To my surprise, she asked me if I would minister to her. Like, wait. Me? She wanted to meet for an hour each week, and just learn more about God. I remember telling Paula about this, and she said that this was the beginning of my ministry. I was nervous, but if this is what God wanted, I was going to do it. By January 2016, we started our weekly meetings. Definitely sought His guidance each time we met. I didn't want to be so excited, and speak from my flesh. I had to remember that this wasn't about me, it was about Jesus. I was just a vessel. God was just aligning things up. The website was coming along, and couldn't wait for it to go up.

A little snag came up. It was time to get the website up, but www.dccreations.com was already taken. What??? And, actually, DC's Creations was taken. Really??? So, I needed a new name. Oh man! I just was not sure what to change it to. Hmmm......still to be about

God's love for women. One day, I went to go visit Paula. We talked for a bit, and I brought up how I needed a new name for the ministry because DC's Creations was already taken. I mentioned that I did not want the ministry to be named after me (with my name), but one that represented who I am. Right away, the Holy Spirit spoke into her and she said, "Why not 'DNC Ministries'. DNC stands for Daughter in Christ, Disciple in Christ. And, it is also a play on your name." I was like, OKAY, GOD!! Here You go!! That's it! Let's move!!!" I quickly sent a text to the young lady about the new name. She said it wasn't taken (of course not. God had that for me). I just needed to get the name registered. I shared the news with James, and he helped me fill out the paperwork. By the end of 2016, DNC Ministries, LLC. was registered. Oh, Lord!! This is exciting and nerve-wracking.

2017 is upon us!!! And you know what? It was time to fast. By this point, I made it a point to fast several times a year, it was really helping me. Now, this one was a bit different. Instead of 21 days, it would be 40 days. Okay.....what now? 40 days? Like, not eat for 40 days, because, I don't know if I can do that. Are we meant to do that? I wasn't expecting this at all, but I know Satan wouldn't tell me to fast for 40 days, let alone to fast at all. So, something had to be up. It was like my 21 day fast, just....longer. During the beginning of the fast, God showed me the same three things: leadership, the ministry and my husband. Now with the husband, I was like, "Where is he, Lord? I've been praying, and everything else." Prayers, yes. Keeping my One true love first, not all of the time. Plus, it wasn't time. I was putting the meeting of my husband above God. God is to be first. He is a jealous God (remember the story of Abraham and Isaac). In Exodus, it states, **"For you shall worship no other god; for the Lord, Whose name is Jealous, is a jealous (impassioned) God," (Exodus 34:14, AMPC).** I was making my future husband a god, and that was not to be. So, pressing in with the fast, the young lady working on the website calls me to set a date to meet up and look over the website. I am so excited!! With the date set, I am anxiously awaiting to see my website. The day is here! I head over to the young lady's place to look at the website. It looks great!! Time to launch it....and it goes live!!! Ahhhh!!! This is happening!!! DNC Ministries, LLC. went live on January 21, 2017!!

With a name change in the ministry, registering the name, officially launching the website and still fasting, February was coming in with more good news. When I fasted the previous year, I fasted social media. It started with six months, then God said the entire year. To be honest, I was fine with that. I was allowing social media, no, giving social media too much power over me. To see friends (past and present) getting into relationships, getting engaged, breaking up, then in another relationship, engaged and then married was getting to me. "Lord, I just want my one husband. Just my one. Am I doing something wrong? Am I not pretty enough? Am I too picky (I mean, just don't be a Patriots fan. There's more, but that's in the top 10)? Am I not out there enough?" All of that went through my mind constantly, so to fast social media for a year, worked for me. But, one was needed for the ministry. Social media was (and primarily is) the way to promote just about anything. Not something I was fond of (still working on it), but wanted to be obedient. So, I created a page for DNC Ministries, LLC. (the Facebook page was created back in 2014 with postings of my artwork). Okay, so we're starting to become more official. This is great! By the time the 40th day arrived for the fast, I was so completely worn out. Talk about weak.....I was so weak.....I literally had the shivers (the last three days were water only). Now, I do not recommend doing a fast for that amount of time, but when God speaks, listen. But, the fast was more for a pain I didn't know I was holding onto.

March 2017, it was on a Sunday (I remember because I attended first service). One of my friends had invited me over for a potluck at her place. Yes, I will be there (I mean.....food, people). As mid-afternoon was approaching, I went into my prayer/war closest. Now, I can say I do not know why, but looking back, I know Who lead me to my prayer/war closest. I was praying for my neighbor, coworkers and whoever else God placed on my heart. Then, I felt tears begin to come to my eyes (like now). I had been studying about forgiveness for the past few months, and.......rcmcmbcr sometime back when Paula asked if I had forgiven my uncle (that was just the beginning). *"But when you are praying, first forgive anyone you are holding a grudge against, so that your Father in heaven will forgive your sins, too."* **(Mark 11:25, NLT**, *emphasis* added). I found myself just starting to cry, first it was soft, and then it picked up. Then, I found myself saying, "I forgive you, dad." Right at that moment, God said, *"Name the offense."* This was something I learned during my study of forgiveness. We are to name the offense so that we can be free, and be no longer connected to that person due to that offense......letting it go (the offense) and not hanging onto that piece that had us angry with that person. So, I yelled out, "I FORGIVE YOU, DAD, FOR REJECTING ME!" I had no idea that was in me, and that's how I felt about my dad. I am still in my prayer/war closest, crying up a storm, then this came out, "I FORGIVE YOU, JASON, FOR RAPING ME!" Oh my goodness! That really happened! I was really raped! "Why did You let it happen, God? (I told myself that it was okay to cry about this as I write it out) Why didn't You save me? You could've stopped him? Take this pain away from me, God. This hurts so much." And, I just sat there.....in my prayer/war closest.....on the floor......letting out tears that I held back.....for years. And, those tears were just the beginning. It was a shock to acknowledge the fact that I was raped. It was shock that it took me 10 years to realize that I was raped. I had no idea that I held that in, and for that long. The lies from the enemy overrode the truth, and I believed those lies. I was angry about that. I remember that I kept saying, "I forgive you, Jason, for raping me. I forgive you, dad, for rejecting me," over and over again. I am not sure how long I was in that room. I was drained. I was so drained from crying and screaming. Okay, Lord. Now, that this has been acknowledged, what do I do?

Like I do, at times, I tried to go back as if nothing happened, but God wasn't going to allow that to happen. This wasn't going to just slide by. Forgiveness is a choice. Forgiveness sets us free. There are so many scriptures about forgiveness. We don't like to forgive, we much rather hang onto the pain (I've mentioned that before). We think that by not forgiving, we are hurting that person, but we are actually only hurting ourselves. I am sure you've heard the saying about drinking bleach (please don't) to kill the other person (something like that), but it actually kills you. **Matthew, Chapter 6** state, "If you *forgive* those who sin against you, your heavenly Father will *forgive* you." **(v.14, NLT)**. Now, this is in red, so you know Jesus is speaking here. And, Jesus forgave while dying on the cross. Did you know that? We like to say that He was fully God, so it was easy for Him to forgive. No, no....that's not true. Jesus is The Word, Himself. He could have easily asked the angels to come down and take Him back up to heaven. But, He knew His purpose. He knew He was sent to live a sinless life, in a sinful world

124

so that we could have an example to follow. He became fully human while praying in the Garden of Gesthamene, asking God to take the cup of suffering away from Him, but said **"....My Father! If this cup cannot be taken away unless I drink it, your will be done." (Matthew 26:42, NLT).** And, He sweated drops of blood He was praying so hard. He saw you and me, and said that we were worth dying on the cross for. Even with the mistakes that we would make (and we will make many), He still chose to sacrifice His life for us, **"For our sake He made Christ [virtually] to be sin Who knew no sin, so that in *and* through Him we might become [endued with, viewed as being in, and example of] the righteousness of God [what we ought to be, approved and acceptable and in right relationship with Him, by His goodness]." (2 Corinthians 5:21 AMP).** Yes, I was hurt physically, emotionally and mentally, but I wasn't sent as a pleasing sacrifice to save the world. Jesus died for me, and forgave me while on the cross. If I am to emulate Him, then I should be able to forgive, and be free. About a week later, I sent a text to my dad. Before you say anything, I did pray about it. The text was about forgiving him for not playing a part in my life. I honestly had no idea how much that affected me. I am sure my dad loves me, he just doesn't know how to show it. And, I forgave him for that. I also said that I would continue to pray for him, and that I was looking forward to the day that he accepts Jesus Christ as his own personal Lord and Savior, and he calls to tell me. That day is coming, I just know it. I felt at peace with that. Now, as for the.......the.....rape.

So, the rape. I was still having a hard time acknowledging that happened to me. Like, the process was........whew....the process. Trying to process all of this. I was really raped? Let me tell you the way I was trying to process it. If I was speaking with a friend, and I brought up about how God was working on me about forgiving, I would say, "I was raped by my ex- boyfriend," and continue with the conversation. It was like me saying, "Girl, I just had mint chocolate chip ice cream." When I would mention it, my friends would be like, "Whoa! What?! Did you say rape?" I would basically skim over it because I was still trying to process it. So, I decided to focus back on the ministry. This will help me get my mind off of the realization that I was raped. I was raped. That played in the back of mind. I was raped.......

Back to DNC Ministries, LLC. Okay, so we have an Instagram page, a website, we're painting, hmmm...something needs to be added. How about to t-shirts? Now, I like t-shirts. I consider myself to be a t-shirt connoisseur. When my favorite artists have new shirts, I will definitely buy like two or three (have to skip the one). How do I go about getting designs and shirts made? My friend, James knew of how to get designs made and who could print the shirts. This was exciting. A flood of designs came to mind. I didn't mention earlier, but a lot of my paintings (canvases, prayer boxes and words of encouragement) have a butterfly on it. God placed this in me some years back. The butterfly represents the new creations we are in Christ. So, I definitely wanted the butterfly to be the symbol for DNC Ministries, LLC. And, I was focusing on the primary colors for the ministry. These are the colors that came to me:

- Purple – represents royalty
- Gold - represents the streets of the New Jerusalem
- Blue – represents the Holy Spirit

Okay, so working on the symbol for the ministry, we have the colors, now what designs are we looking at. The first design was from one of my favorite scriptures, **Psalm 46:10**, "Be Still and know that I am God." Next one up, 'Jesus, You are Worth The Risk.' That one came up while doing a Bible App devotional about living a life unashamed for Jesus. I also wanted to have a logo on my shirts, so I came up, no the Holy Spirit, came up with the design. My initial 'D,' at the bottom of the letter is a caterpillar (that's how we start out), then the center would represent the chrysalis (this is where we allow God to remove the filth from us; shame, guilt, condemnation, idolatry, sexual immorality, lying, stealing, greed, adultery, lust, depression, addiction, etc..) then out of the other end is a butterfly (this represents who we become once we emerge from the chrysalis). I couldn't believe what the Holy Spirit revealed to me. I shared it with James, and we sent the design to the print shop so that it could be on all of the shirts! Oh boy!! This is big!!! The next shirt, 'I live Passionately for Jesus because He died Passionately for me,' came from how we should live our lives for Jesus. His death was so passionate, and it was for us, so we should live so passionately for Him while here on earth (this is my everyday goal). Now, one of my favorite designs came from one of my paintings,

'Fearfully and Wonderfully Made.' I know most of us know **Psalm 139:14**. Here it is in several different versions:

"I will confess and praise You *for You are fearful and wonderful and* for the awful wonder of my birth! Wonderful are Your works, and that my inner self knows right well." **(Psalm 139:14,** AMP)

"I will praise you because I have been remarkably and wondrously made. Your works are wondrous, and I know this very well." **(Psalm 139:14,** CSB)

"I praise you because I am fearfully and wonderfully made; your works are wonderful, I know that full well." **(Psalm 139:14**, NIV)

"Thank you for making me so wonderfully complex! Your workmanship is marvelous- how well I know it." **(Psalm 139:14**, NLT)

Four different versions, saying the same thing, in their own way. But, do understand what they are saying? I mean, I didn't. I just quoting scripture, not fully understanding what I was saying. God made me, so fearful, so wonderful, so remarkable, so wondrous, and so complex! God's workmanship, me, is so marvelous and wonderful, that my inner self knows this, and will praise and confess this to everyone I know. Now, when I say, 'I am fearfully and wonderfully made' it has a different meaning. Man, I am so thankful that the Holy Spirit gives clarity to The Bible when we ask. Another design that came to mind was, 'Jesus did not save you to be silent' with a cross in the center. This one hit hard, but I suppressed it. I just didn't want to face what happened to me. Despite that, 2017 was a great year....I guess you could say.

Can you believe its 2018?! Well, DNC Ministries, LLC. is going well. I mean, there were some shakeups. The young lady who started the website was not able to work it anymore because she was getting busy. I didn't want to give up, so I created a website on my own. Now, it was nothing the way the young lady had it, but, I didn't want to give up on the ministry (I was starting to feel a bit discouraged). I had shirts and paintings, yet no one was buying. I was even posting on social media, and that wasn't working. Was I not posting correctly? How many hashtags do I need? 10, 20, 50? How often do I need to post? Every two seconds? Lord, is this worth it? Now, I was still praying for my husband, I wasn't seeing results. What do I need to do? I started to find myself praying differently for my husband. I was asking God to help me be a better communicator, especially when it came to disagreements. At times, I would close up, but I believe that my future husband would not let me just stew and be upset, but actually call me out (in a loving way), and hold me accountable to actually share (in a loving way) whatever I would be upset about. Communication is so important, and I definitely was praying for that between my husband and me. I also found myself praying not to bring baggage into our relationship. Whatever was holding me back from being free, to help release it to God. You're probably wondering, "Didn't she forgive her dad and ex-boyfriend last year?" I was still suppressing the rape, and didn't realize it. I knew that I didn't want to put pressure on my future husband, or respond a certain way whenever he would touch me. I also wasn't realizing why this would come up so often.

I did share with a few more friends about being raped, but my delivery needed work. I would skim over it, and keep talking about something else. One weekend, during the summer of 2018, my mom stayed a weekend with me. We were eating dinner at the table, and we were just talking. She shared something personal with me, and talked of how God was helping her to acknowledge it. I was wanting to have a deep conversation with my mom, so I shared with her about being raped. It was hard for me because this was the relationship I lied to her about. She looked at me, and said, "That explains you dress the way you do." I was floored!!!!! WHAT?! I asked what she meant by that. She talked about how I wear tank tops and shorts (we live in Florida, so......), my dresses and how I carried myself in general. I was completely in shock, but didn't know how not to yell, I mean, she is my mom. I explained to her that my tank tops were not revealing, nor were my shorts that short. I explained that my dresses were not revealing, nor inappropriate to wear to work or church. Because of the rape, I became more self-conscious with how I looked and what I wore. I was so hurt and angry, but couldn't express it in a healthy way. That wasn't the answer I was expecting from my mom. She didn't ask how I felt, or if I reported it to the police. She just.....judged me. My own mom. But, God revealed to me how she was hurting and to give grace and forgive her for the response she gave me. She was coming from a place of hurt. So, I had a choice, do I forgive her or hang on to the hurt of her words? Forgiveness is a choice..........I chose to forgive her.

"Be gentle *and* forbearing with one another and, if one has a difference (a grievance or complaint) against another, readily pardoning each other; even as the Lord has [freely] forgiven you, so must you also [forgive]." **(Colossians 3:13 AMP)**

New Creation

"Therefore if any person is [ingrafted] in Christ (the Messiah) (s)he is a new creation (a new creature altogether); the old [previous moral and spiritual condition] has passed away. Behold, the fresh and new has come!" **(2 Corinthians 5:17,** *AMP, (s) added)*

"For we are God's [own] handiwork (His workmanship), recreated in Christ Jesus, [born anew] that we may do those good works which God predestined (planned beforehand) for us [taking paths which He prepared ahead of time], that we should walk in them [living the good life which He prearranged and made ready for us to live.]" **(Ephesians 2:10,** *AMP)*

So, I forgave my mom for her......her......response.....lack of reaction.......either way, I forgave her. It was painful for me because even though I had forgiven Jason for what he did to me, I was still feeling guilty. Yes, I was praying for my future husband (even tried on bridal dresses in 2018, because that's how much faith I have that he's on his way), but I was beginning to wonder if he would love me once he found out about the rape. Would he want to touch me? Do I want him touching me? And, I mean, intimately. Holding hands is one thing, but to be intimate with another man, even though I had been violated......would that cause a rift between us? I didn't want any of that. I wanted to let it go, but......

I remember I met up with a friend from church one Saturday for lunch. We ate at Chuy's (if you have never been before.....what are you waiting for. And, please get the Creamy Jalapeno Dip, better known as "The Crack Dip." That's what I call it). We were on the patio talking and eating, and I just happened to share that I was raped, and kept on talking. She was like, "Hold up. Back up. What did you just say?" I was like, "Oh yeah, I need to get better at sharing that. But, yes, I was raped by my ex-boyfriend over 11 years ago." I admitted that how I said it was like non-chalant, but the truth was, I was still numb from it. I believe that is why I would say it the way I would, because I was still numb from the acknowledgment of being raped. And, how long it took me to actually realize it. I had forgiven him, but not myself. Plus, I didn't want the 'pity look.' The, 'Oh, I am so sorry," look. She allowed me to share my story (I didn't want this to be my story). She didn't judge me. She didn't look down on me. She told me that by looking at me, no one would've ever thought I went through something so traumatic. She said that it shocked her because she wasn't expecting that. And, how cheerful of a person I am, that she wasn't expecting it. Anyone can hide behind a smile. I didn't cry while I was telling her. I didn't want to cry about it anymore. I just wanted it to go away. I mean, I forgive him, so why bring it up anymore?

I put my focus back into DNC Ministries, LLC. Oh, yes!! I created an Etsy Shop for my artwork, InspiredbyHISWORD (God's Word is a sword (look up Hebrews 4:12)). Paula helped me come with that name. She's really good at that. So, now I have an Etsy Shop for my artwork, an Instagram page for DNC Ministries, LLC., shirts for the ministry and an updated Facebook page, and still.......slow moving. "Lord, You showed me that I would be speaking in front of women, sharing The Word and speaking of Your goodness. But, nothing is happening. No one is buying anything. I am not getting a lot of likes on my pages. I am not getting a lot of followers. What's the point?" Ever have those moments? The "God You said" moments? If not, then you may want to check your relationship with the Lord, because you will have plenty of those. Have those honest moments with the Lord. He can take it. We serve a BIG God! Now, I was trying to get to the end result, but I still needed to go through the journey (the part we don't like).

Talk about a journey. Remember when I became a lead in the Hospitality department at church? Well, that was a journey. One God would use in a BIG way. So, you know this mouth I keep telling you about, more like the tongue, just needed to be tamed. Plus, my attitude and disposition needed to change. From 2011-2016.....let me tell you. Actually, I'll share what I wrote to my pastor and the leads over me back on March 25, 2018. Backstory real quick, each year (since I've been attending) the church has a 'Volunteer Appreciation Lunch.' It would typically be on a Sunday (after church), and it always seemed to land on a Sunday where I served all day. Not that I didn't want to go, but my fur baby wouldn't make it 9-10 hours by himself, so I wouldn't attend. Plus, who's voting for me (each department at church would pick someone who they thought was growing throughout that year).

Well, God worked it to where it would be held on a Friday night. Yeah, God is something. So, I did attend in 2018, and here's the part where I share what I wrote:

Hello!!

First, I hope you are having a wonderful weekend! Second, I apologize for sending this, like about two months late (God has been pressing this on me for a bit).

I wanted to say, "Thank you!" This comes about because I was (and still am) shocked that I was chosen to receive the Spirit Award for the Hospitality Department. I will share why.

This woman right here, Danielle, has been through quite a bit since being a member and serving at church. I already know God has given me a heart to serve, so that wasn't an issue. Really, it was where God placed me to serve. I love people, but at times....well, the flesh was ruling quite a bit. I was fine with serving in the Hospitality Department, but (due to living far from church) I requested to not setup on Saturdays. Once it became official that we had to setup on Saturdays if we were serving on Sundays, I allowed Satan to completely come in and take over. I had attitude whenever I came to setup (I was very blatant about it), which would carry over into Sunday.

Now, that doesn't mix...attitude and serving??? For real, Danielle?! Obviously, I was fighting something. I would want to leave the Hospitality Department and serve somewhere else. I was upfront and honest about it.

Next thing I know, I am being asked to be a lead. Really??? Are we not seeing the attitude and demeanor? I mean, it's all over my face. I was taken aback about this because I was not sure why they would want me to be a lead. So, I stepped into the position, and about few months in, I had attitude again. Now, by this point, I thought I would be asked to step down.....or something. No, whatever I was trying (rather what Satan was trying) to manipulate, God had other plans.

I remember praying one morning on the way to church (to serve) and asking the Lord to reveal to me why I was behaving this way. Why did I have a chip on my shoulder? And to who? God revealed to me that

I was afraid of stepping into a position that I was created to be in......a leader (I am literally crying while typing this). God revealed to me that I have a tendency to fight when I am afraid and not trusting in Him. I get caught up with, "who am I to be the one to lead someone in the Hospitality Department....or, anywhere?" That's not my call. I also realized that God was using the ladies in the Hospitality Department to confirm what He had been telling me I would hear that I am a great leader, a natural leader and how much the ladies enjoyed serving with me (even with my attitude and negative disposition). It blew me away, humbled me, and had me repenting. I wanted to become a better leader and stop fighting what God had for me. Once that happened, God moved in a BIG way!! I also became a trainer. A little more responsibility, which can also mean more stress. Not realizing it then, but I was being tested. The coffee pot wouldn't work, the iPad wouldn't play music, or someone would come in late. At first, Satan was winning those battles. I would be stressed and it would show. One day, I asked the Lord why was this happening to me. God said, *"why not you?"* I was not digging that answer, but I knew there was a reason.....a purpose. So, instead of complaining or being upset, I would thank the Lord for being with me, providing me this opportunity and for guiding the day. I started quoting **Psalm 19:14**, "May the words of my mouth and the meditation of my heart be pleasing to you, O LORD, my rock and my redeemer." (NLT). I noticed a change that day. Satan couldn't get to me because I was changing my mind set and allowing God to move and work in me.

Then, another shake up takes place. The young lady who was overseeing the Hospitality Department was promoted into another position, so now a new person will take over. WHAT? Someone new? But, I am used to the other young lady. She was used to my attitudes. Right away, the flesh wanted to take over. But, God had other plans. The new person's first day was on a Sunday I was leading. I remember going up to her, welcoming her and telling her that if she needed anything, we were all there to help. She told me she was nervous at first, but felt at peace knowing I was on the team. Why did that shake me? In a good way? I wasn't expecting that. This is really all God.

Here we go, another shake up. We are moving into our new church home and God presses more than ever into my being that I am going to serve, serve, and serve. I had no idea that I would go from not wanting to setup on Saturdays, to serving just about every Sunday. Where did this come from?

So, we come to January 2018. The Volunteer Appreciation Dinner. While sitting at the table with a few friends, one of them kept telling me that I would be getting the Spirit Award for Hospitality. I was like, "No, I have a mouth still. Another lead in our department will get it because she truly gives and gives." My friend kept saying it would be me. I didn't believe it. Our Senior Lead gets up to speak (she loves doing that) and then I hear my name.....'Danielle Cador.' WHAT?! ME?! REALLY?! Blown away! What really blew me was the reception I received. I had no idea that people felt that way about me. The reception was so loud and loving.....I actually cried on the way home when it all came back to mind. Me??? When I came into church the following Sunday, people were still congratulating me and telling me it was well- deserved. WOW! That is when it all hit me. God placed me in the Hospitality Department for a reason. I spent a few years fighting it because I didn't want to see it.

Being in the Hospitality Department has really played a big part in my walk with the Lord. Allowing Him to prune me, purify me, humble me, teach me, work in and through me, shape me, mold me....and it is still happening.....I'm just learning to not be stubborn about it. I thank you so much for seeing in me what I couldn't see in me. For not giving up on me and listening to the Lord. I share this story with quite a few people because I am seeing the transformation. I am thankful for where God has me at this church. I am right where I need to be and I am growing.

Thank you and love you,

Danielle

That was the email I sent to the pastor and leaders of the Hospitality Department. And, it was all true. Honestly, the email could have gone on for days, but I just wanted to get to the main points. God certainly used those years, and in that particular department, to work on me. Now, the mouth is still there, but the serving just continued to increase. I believe I served for like, six months straight from the time it was close to move into our new church, and afterwards. I had people calling or text me asking if I was serving. They wanted to make sure that I was getting The Word, as well as serving.

2018 continued to move. I wanted to see more movement out of DNC Ministries, LLC. I was feeling as if I hit the low point in the ministry, because I wasn't moving in the timeframe I thought I should've been moving. I would sell a shirt or two. A painting or two. I even started blogging. No one was reading those (that I could see). I started a study on The Book of Psalm. A chapter a day, and talk about what God was saying, and how it pertains to our walk today. No one was interested (that I could see). I wanted fast movement in the ministry, and......my husband. We know that's never how God works. It's never our timing, it's His. We just want His timing to align with ours, am I right? And, God showed me the ministry, how far it would go, and so on. "Why is this not happening now, Lord? You see that I have shirts....the designs You showed me. You know I am not that good at creating a website, why haven't You sent anyone my way to help? You say I have not because I ask not." Now, that scripture, we twist around a lot. We need to read the verses before the main one (you know I like the Amplified Version),

"What leads to strife (discord and feuds) and how do conflicts (quarrels and fightings) originate among you? Do they not arise from your sensual desires that are ever warring in your bodily members? You are jealous and covet [what others have] and your desires go unfulfilled; [so] you become murderers. [To hate is to murder as far as your hearts are concerned.] You burn with envy and anger and are not able to obtain [the gratification, the contentment, and the happiness that you seek], so you fight and war. You do not have, because you do not ask. [I John 3:15]. [Or] you do ask [God for them] and yet fail to receive, because you ask with wrong purpose and evil, selfish motives. Your intention is [when you get what you desire] to spend it in sensual pleasures." **(James 4:1-3,** AMPC).

Now, I would highlight, underline and all of that, but all of this hit home for me. When the Holy Spirit led me to these verses, I was like, "Just slay me, Lord!! Oh, You did that?! Okay, then let me just lay here, on my face, for like six months." I am asking about growth in my ministry, but am I asking out of selfish motive? Am I wanting to be 'seen, 'or am

I wanting God to be seen? Am I going to push God to the side when my husband comes into the picture, brag about him in a selfish way? Or, am I going to praise and thank God each day for the ministry that He's given me? Praise and thank Him for the man of God He's placed in my life? Allow God to use my journey to encourage, heal, draw women to Jesus and He becomes their own personal Lord and Savior, and live the life of freedom that Jesus died for them to have? Will I allow God to walk me through this process....step by step....no matter how long it takes, to get me to where He needs me to be fully for Him? Am I willing to be a one woman show during this season, to draw closer to Him and allow Him to do what He needs to do in me? We are about to find out.

2018 was a good year, but 2019 was about to be.....a game changer. By this time, I've told a few friends about.....being raped (still hard to wrap my brain around). One weekend in January, a friend stayed over for the weekend. We started talking, and she said that God revealed something about me to her. I wasn't surprised because I knew God wanted to tell me something (don't ask me how I knew). She wrote it down in her journal, and shared it with me. Now, I am going to share it with you:

Let Danielle know that I have set her free from the rape that happened to her and that she is worthy. Let her know that she needs to unpack it because the enemy is trying to use it against her and it's making her (portraying) her a certain way. Tell her to put down the walls and the guard that she thinks has been protecting her from being hurt, I have her heart and will not allow her to be hurt, but she needs to talk about it and be healed in order to bring others out. It is not her fault. God is delivering her from a spirit of rejection. Do not be ashamed about what happened. That is not her identity. I am her father and she is my daughter. It's ok for her to cry and show her emotions and feel hurt about what happened. Tell her to tell me how she feels about it. If she is upset with me about it then I want her to tell me. I want her to get it all out. When she gets past and gives it to me, I will send her husband. I don't want her entering into the relationship with that pain and feeling like she can't trust who I am sending to her. I saw her faith in preparing for a husband. She was not crazy and that I see and understand what she was doing. Let her know the scriptures **James 2:26** faith without works is dead and **Hebrews 11:1, 6**

That was the message from God that my friend was to give to me. All of that was on point. Very accurate. I knew it was real, but when she got to the part of God seeing what I did in preparing for my husband, I was blown away!! I never told her what I did. I only told my mom, and she thought I was crazy. Remember when I said that I tried on bridal dresses? I did that in the summer of 2018. A dear friend went with me to a bridal store, so I could try on dresses. I was preparing. God saw that!! He sees everything, but for Him to mention that to her and relay it to me....oh my goodness!!! I did have walls up. I didn't want to be hurt again. I was scared of who God would bring into my life because of the lack of trust I had in God. I knew Satan was trying to use the rape against me. The enemy wanted the rape to be my identity. While she was speaking this, God gave me a vision: in the middle of my chest was a big, huge gaping wound, with blood streaming down. I kept putting band aids on the wound, hoping the pain would go away, but they would fall off because of all of the blood streaming down. God wanted to take my wound, the painful wound and turn it into a beautiful scar. He actually put His finger on my wound. He wanted to turn what Satan meant for harm into good for Him. To bring Him glory. Did you read the part about bringing others out? God told Moses that he was the one to lead the Israelites out of Egypt and into the Promised Land. I am the one God chose to help bring women out of their shame, guilt, rejection. Then, it came to me like a freight train.....DNC Ministries, LLC. is about helping women see their worth in Jesus, in the midst of their pain. To help them realize that the sexual assault that took place against them was not their fault, and that God sees them, not the assault. That He loves them with so much abandon, He gave up His only Son to prove it. That we are Victorious, not victims. Satan wants us to feel like victims, to feel broken, to feel as if we are unwanted. But, God does want us. He created us for Him. Rejection doesn't come from our Abba, Father (I heard Him tell me that I hadn't called Him that in a while. Brought tears to my eyes). And, God is using me....little 'ole, spit-fire me. All of that took my breath away. And, I wanted to be healed, not to meet my husband, but to be healed for Jesus. To be free from the shackles Satan has tried to keep around my ankles and wrists. I wasn't claiming the rape, I was claiming my victory over the rape. God wants that for you, too. Here are some scriptures to help you live a victorious life:

"This is my command – be strong and courageous! Do not be afraid or discouraged. For the LORD your God is with you wherever you go." (Joshua 1:9, NLT) (posted in my bathroom)

"Create in me a clean heart, O God, and renew a right spirit within me. Cast me not away from your presence, and take not your Holy Spirit from me. Restore to me the joy of your salvation, and uphold me with a willing spirit." (Psalm 51:10-12, English Standard Version (ESV))

"I beseech you therefore, brethren (and sisters), by the mercies of God that ye present your bodies a living sacrifice, holy, acceptable unto God, which is your reasonable service. And be not conformed to this world: but be ye transformed by the renewing of your mind, that ye may prove what is that good, and acceptable, and perfect will of God." (Romans 12:1-2, King James Version (KJV), added with emphasis)

"And He died for all, so that all those who live might live no longer to and for themselves, but to and for Him Who died and was raised again for their sake." (2 Corinthians 5:15, AMPC)

"Do not fret or have any anxiety about anything, but in every circumstances and in everything, by prayer and petition (definite requests), with thanksgiving, continue to make your wants known to God. And God's peace [shall be yours, that tranquil state of a soul assured of its salvation through Christ, and so fearing nothing from God and being content with its earthly lot of whatever sort that is, that peace] which transcends all understanding shall garrison and mount guard over your hearts and minds in Christ Jesus. For the rest, brethren, whatever is true, whatever is worthy of reverence and is honorable and seemly, whatever is just, whatever is pure, whatever is lovely and lovable, whatever is kind and winsome and gracious, if there is any virtue and excellence, if there is anything worthy of praise, think on and weigh and take account of these things [fix your minds on them]." (Philippians 4:6-8, AMPC) (I cling to these).

"Yet I will rejoice in the Lord; I will exult in the [victorious] God of my salvation! [Romans 8:37]. The Lord God is my Strength, my personal bravery, and my invincible army; He makes my feet like hinds' feet and will make me to walk [not to stand still I terror, but to walk] and make [spiritual] progress upon my high places [of trouble, suffering, or responsibility]!" **(Habakkuk 3:18-19, AMP)**

Remember my mom's response when I told her I was raped? I was speaking with a co-worker (we were talking about our growth in the Lord, and other topics). I shared with her about me being raped (Starting to get better with my delivery). She was shocked! I started to cry a little. She asked if I told my mom about it, and I shared my mom's response. I broke down at my desk. I didn't want it to bother me when my mom said it back in 2018, but I also wanted to throw up my wall.....my defense mechanism. This time, it came back to mind, and it hurt me so much. I didn't know how to handle my mom's response. I knew it hurt me back then, but....this was different. It was traumatizing. Right up there with being raped. This was another area that needed to be healed. After work, I went into my prayer closest, and asked the Lord to help me, truly help me, forgive my mom. I know God is going to use this pain as well. Giving it all to you, Lord.

Now, remember I mentioned earlier that God told me that I would be going out speaking and sharing His Word? I held my first seminar in April 2019. It was called, 'Glorifying God in My Pain.' That was the first time, I publicly started sharing what happened to me. I cried in front of the ladies, but that meant I was healing. A woman attending the seminar was healed that day. She was able to forgive her abuser and fully seek the love of God. "Okay God. I see what You're doing." Still wanted to see the ministry grow through leaps and bounds, but there's a process. I held my second seminar in October 2019 titled, 'Who Said? Whose Voice are You Listening To?' I taught about the 12 spies going to the land of Canaan, and 10 coming back with the negative report, and two having a positive report. The ten didn't make it to the Promised Land (you can read more in Numbers 13 and 14). God started to have women seek me out. I was asked to be on a Women's panel in November 2019. We talked about putting on band aids when we should let the wound fully heal. There was a moment where the Pastor shared amazing insight, and I was secretly hoping I would be skipped to speak. The moderator started a new topic, and started with me, but then the Pastor said, "Unless you have something to say about the last topic." I knew that was the Holy Spirit wanting me to speak up. So, I shared my story. It was hard, but like the Lord told my friend, I needed to speak about it, in order to be healed. After the panel, women were coming up to me saying how brave I was for sharing my story, and how much women need to hear it so that they can be healed. All confirmation from the Lord.

I am still in the process of healing. I know the seminars and panels were just the beginning of all God has in store. He had me start a podcast called, 'The Butterfly Effect.' There, I share my story, and remind women of their worth in Jesus by discussing different topics, such as, purity in a relationship, purity while not in a relationship, enjoy the season of singleness, friendships, serving God, loving our hair and more. It's another platform God has given me. It's also to prepare for what else He has. Now, I didn't see myself writing a book, but can I tell you, writing this book has been huge because I am sharing my story on a different level. There are times I still cry, and I know I will cry when I tell another woman about being raped, but I will also cry when I share that accepting Jesus as my personal Lord and Savior was the best decision I made in my life. And, knowing that God loves me, flaws and all, and that He is my Father, something worth crying over as well. This isn't the end for me, it's just the beginning. I am excited to see what else is on the horizon, not only for me, but for DNC Ministries, LLC. Remember the scriptures that God told my friend to tell me, I will share them with you:

"Just as the body is dead without breath, so also faith is dead without works." (James 2:26, NLT).

"NOW FAITH is the assurance (the confirmation, the title deed) of the things [we] hope for, being the proof of things [we] do not see and the conviction of their reality [faith perceiving as real fact what is not revealed to the senses]." (Hebrews 11:1, AMPC)

"Now without faith it is impossible to please God, for the one who draws near to Him must believe that He exists and rewards those who seek Him." (Hebrews 11:6, HCSB)

Faith is a spiritual gift. There's the gift of salvation (knowing that Jesus saved you), but there's the gift of faith where one believes what God said. This person takes God at His Word and put their entire weight of their lives in His hands. She expects God to move. I have been given this gift. I knew I had it, but my pastor pointed it out to me one Sunday after service. At first, I was like no, then I realized I do. Remember, I am preparing for my husband, but I know God will present him in His timing. And, I trust God's timing. He's not failed me before. That's what He wants you, woman of God, to remember and cling to. He's never failed you before, so He won't do so now. He loves you. He's wild about you. You're His. Doesn't that bring tears to your eyes? It does for me, every time.

I wanted to share with you my playlist. I love praise and worship. It's awesome seeing the Holy Spirit move. These are the songs that I go back to over and over, and they have helped me so much. If you get a chance, listen to the words of the songs, and listen for God's voice. Allow the Holy Spirit to open your eyes, heart, mind, ears and soul while listening to the songs. You will receive so much revelation of the freedom God wants to bring you. I'll have those at the end of the book. It's just a few them. Some songs are classics. Some are new, which will turn into classics (at least for me). Each of them bring tears to my heart and eyes. Music is another way God speaks to me. At times, I feel as if the songs were written just for me. Ever experience that? Most of the time, the songs are things I've wanted to say, or how I've felt, but couldn't get the words out. And, the Holy Spirit just moves in such a way when I worship to these songs, the words pouring out what I feel, but not able to say them in an articulate manner. But, the Holy Spirit knows what I am feeling and praying, so he takes my jumbled words, fixes them accordingly and lays them at God's feet. I pray that the songs bring healing to your heart, mind, body, soul and emotions. The playlist is available on Spotify, 'Danielle's Playlist.'

I pray that this book helps you, in a way that you can give your past hurts and pains to the One Who wants to take them from you. Meditate on **1 Peter 5:7**, cast your cares upon him. He doesn't want you carrying the weight your shoulders were never meant to carry. That's why He sent His Son, Jesus. Let God heal that wound, so you can be free. He wants to do a new thing in you **(Isaiah 43:18-19)**, so you can rest in Him **(Matthew 11:28-30)**. Jesus is everything, but if you need someone to talk to, make sure you seek out someone with godly wisdom and godly counsel. Always ask the Holy Spirit for discernment when seeking for a therapist, psychiatrist and counselor. And, there's nothing wrong with doing so. I am praying for you, sweet friend. You're not on this journey alone. Jesus is walking with you, and I am walking with you too. It's time to spread your wings and become the butterfly you were created to be, but first, you have to let God mold you while you're in the chrysalis. It hurts, but it is so worth it......you are so worth it. Your journey isn't over.....it's just beginning.

Lord, I pray that every woman that has read this book, understands that You've never abandoned them. You've never turned Your back on them, because that's not Who You are. You are a loving God, a loving Father, One Who doesn't like to see His children in pain......any pain. It hurts You to see Your daughters suffer. It hurt You to see Your Son, Jesus, crucified on the cross, but he needed to be sacrificed to save us. I know You hear the cries of Your children, for they do not fall on deaf ears. I pray that each person allows You to do a mighty work in them. That they see You wanting to do a new thing in and through them, but that they first need to give their pain over to You, the One Who wants to heal them from the inside out. You are our Jehovah-Rophe (Almighty Healer), and You can breathe healing into every soul. May they allow You to turn their wounds into beautiful scars to be used to bring glory to Your name and Kingdom. In Jesus' Name. Amen (so be it).

PRAYER OF SALVATION

The most beautiful and important relationship to have and desire, is to have a deep, intimate, personal relationship with the One Who gave up His life for you, Jesus Christ. If you would like to receive Jesus as your personal Lord and Savior and have that special relationship like no other, please pray this prayer below:

Father,

You showed Your love for the world by sending Your One and Only Begotten Son to save it. To die for our sins so that whoever believes in Him shall not perish and have eternal life.

We are saved by grace through faith, which is a gift from You. And, there's nothing we can do to earn it.

Your Word says that if I openly declare that Jesus is Lord and believe in my heart that You raised Your Son, Jesus Christ, from the dead and that He is the Savior of the world. And, that He died on the cross for me, which bore all of my sins, paying the price, then I am saved.

Lord, I believe in my heart that You did raise Jesus Christ from the dead and that He is alive today.

I confess that I am sinner, and I am sorry for my sins. I do ask for Your forgiveness. May I freely accept and receive Your forgiveness of my sins. By faith, I do accept and receive Your Son, Jesus Christ, as my personal Lord and Savior into my life. I am saved and will spend forever in eternity with You! I am truly grateful, Abba, Father, for welcoming me with open arms into Your Kingdom! In Jesus' Name, Amen (so be it!).

WELCOME TO THE FAMILY!

REFLECTION

You smile when you realize that God has truly been for you, not against you. You smile when you truly understand that God wants to take the gaping wound you've been carrying around for years, the wound you've been trying to cover with band aids, but they kept falling off, the wound that you wanted to cling so deeply to, but realized that it was holding you back. God wants to heal that wound, your heart, your mind and your soul. He wants to turn that wound into a beautiful scar...for Him...for others. You smile when you realize that you don't have to run anymore. You don't have to hide, or try to be someone He didn't create you to be.

God was always chasing my heart, but I didn't know that. I didn't know that when, years ago, I decided to be called, 'Dani,' that I was actually running from the One Who could save me...the One Who did save me. If you only knew what all 'Dani' endured...if you only knew.

In 2012, God called me by my name, 'Danielle,' and told me to continue to serve Him. That was the first time I heard His audible voice. I said 'yes' to Him. Accepted Jesus as my personal Lord and Savior in February 2009. I was shook then, and again when He called me by my name. He knows my name! In 2014-2015, a shifting was taking place. For the first time in...20 plus years, I decided to fully walk in my name, 'Danielle.' I had friends excited for me to fully walk in my name, others...either chose not to understand, or just really didn't understand. Calling a person by their name says who they are (checkout Abram, Sarai, Jacob, Saul and Simon...). For years, I was afraid of being who God called me to be, but that was falling to the wayside. You see, Satan will use people to try to hold you back, to keep you from your purpose. I felt like I had to explain why I chose to walk in my name. Back in the day, the only time I heard my name called, was if my mom was upset with me. But, after hearing my Abba, Father call me by my name, my perspective changed. It took me awhile to even get used to calling myself by my name, Danielle. There are some that still try to call me 'Dani' but I am learning not to respond because that was my past. Old habits are hard to let go of, but we can let this go. Trying to call me by the past will get you no response. I won't let Satan hold me back any longer. I am a new creation! I can smile about that! The work God is doing in and through me...WON'T HE DO IT!

You can smile when you realize that Danielle is the daughter of a King, a new creation, child of the Most High, Redeemed, Forgiven, Worthy, Adored, Chosen, Loved.....HIS. You can smile when you realize that Danielle is walking in her purpose, mission, calling and destiny.

I can smile...because...I am Danielle!

Danielle is Hebrew, and the female variant of the name Daniel, meaning "God is my judge."

ABOUT THE AUTHOR

Danielle Cador is the founder of a women's ministry, DNC Ministries, LLC (Daughter in Christ, Disciple in Christ). The ministry was founded in 2016. Danielle wanted more of God's heart, and He showed her that women need to truly know Whose they are, in the midst of pain (rape, verbal abuse, molestation, physical assault (sexual), rejection, abandonment, etc....). A reminder that the sexual assault is not their identity, because their identity is in Christ. God wants to take those wounds, the deep painful wounds, and turn them into beautiful scars to be used for Him. DNC Ministries, LLC. is a safe place, safe space, where women can share their journey. Danielle teaches about healing through her own personal experience, The Bible and God. She continues to share this passion on her podcast, The Butterfly Effect Podcast, which airs every Wednesday night on all available platforms.

Danielle attended Regis University in Colorado Springs, Co. and received her Bachelors of Science in Marketing/Management with a Minor in Spanish, and a Master's Degree in International Business with a Minor in Communications.

She is an avid reader, enjoys traveling, spending time with family and friends, eat good cuisine, a **MARVEL** fan and enjoys the beach. She lives in Florida and is a mom to a spunky Bichon Frise.

Danielle travels and speaks and shares with women at seminars, women's panels, women's conferences, and high schools all over the world.

Connect with her on social media:

Instagram:
@dnc_ministries, @the_butterfly_effect_3, @monarchbutterfly_20 and @inspiredbyhiswod
Facebook: DNC Ministries, LLC. (@butterflyDNC)
Website: www.dnc.ministries.com
Email: Dncministriesllc@gmail.com

Book Discussion: Monarchbutterflypublishing@gmail.com

The Butterfly Effect

For Bookings and Public Speakings, Send request to: Improverbs3130@gmail.com

You can order a shirt at: https://goinkit.com/DNC_Ministries/shop/home

Checkout my Shopify Store: https://chrysalistowings.com

Be sure to tune in to The Butterfly Effect Podcast every Wednesday night @ 9PM/EST. Available on Apple, Google, Spotify, Stitcher and more. New episode every week!

DANIELLE'S PLAYLIST

1) Praise You in This Storm by Casting Crowns

2) Beautiful Exchange by Hillsong Worship

3) As You Find Me by Hillsong UNITED

4) Known by Tauren Wells

5) Like Incense/Sometimes by Step by Hillsong Worship

6) Sails by Pat Barrett feat. Steffany Gretzinger and Amanda Cook

7) I Don't Need You by Andy Mineo

8) The Father's House by Cory Asbury

9) I Surrender by Hillsong Worship

10) Speak the Name by Koryn Hawthorne feat. Natalie Grant (2018 Dove Award Performance)

11) Waymaker by Sinach

12) Nothing Else by Cody Carnes

13) Even When It Hurts (Praise Song) by Hillsong UNITED

14) Step Into Love by Tedashii feat. Sarah Reeves

15) Not in a Hurry by Will Reagan and United Pursuit

16) Build My Life by Pat Barrett

17) God Only Knows by IV King and Country

18) What a Beautiful Name by Hillsong Worship

19) Won't He Do It by Koryn Hawthorne

20) Clarity by Andy Mineo

21) Egypt by Bethel Music feat. Cory Asbury

22) Champion by Bethel Music feat. Dante Bowe

23) So Will I (100 Billion X) by Hillsong UNITED

24) Raise a Hallelujah by Bethel Music feat. Jonathan David and Melissa Helser

25) Nobody by Casting Crowns feat. Matthew West

26) The God Who Stays by Matthew West

27) Highlands (Song of Ascent) by Hillsong UNITED

28) Is He Worthy? by Chris Tomlin

29) God's Not Done With You by Tauren Wells

30) Catch the Wind by Jonathan David and Melissa Helser

31) Who You Say I Am by Hillsong Worship

32) History by Bethel Music feat. Alton Eugene

33) Be Still by Hillsong Worship

34) This Love by Housefires

35) Goodness of God by Bethel Music feat. Jenn Johnson

36) Surrounded (Fight My Battles) - UPPERROOM

37) Oh My Soul by Casting Crowns

38) I Ain't Done by Andy Mineo

39) Sweet Victory by Trip Lee

40) Refiner by Maverick City TRIBL Music feat. Chandler Moore and Steffany Gretzinger

41) My Weapon (Sacred Version) by Natalie Grant

42) Shoulders by IV King and Country

43) Respond by Travis Greene (feat. Trinity Anderson, D-Nar Young, Taylor Poole)

44) Haven't Seen It Yet by Danny Gokey

https://open.spotify.com/playlist/6hob3FLQdmgCaWdyuduvun?si=zxIYx5_rQi6PzuBSEZ8FTw

Available on Spotify

SCRIPTURES TO SPEAK OUT DURING SPIRITUAL WARFARE

In conclusion, be strong in the Lord [be empowered through your union with Him]; draw your strength from Him [that strength which His boundless might provides].

Put on God's whole armor [the armor of a heavy-armed soldier which God supplies], that you may be able successfully to stand up against [all] the strategies *and* the deceits of the devil. For we are not wrestling with flesh blood [contending only with physical opponents], but against the despotisms, against the powers, against [the master spirits who are] the world rulers of this present darkness, against the spirit forces of wickedness in the heavenly (supernatural) sphere.

Therefore put on God's complete armor, that you may be able to resist *and* stand your ground on the evil day [of danger], and having done all [the crisis demands], to stand [firmly in your place].

Stand therefore [hold your ground], having tightened the bel of truth around your loins and having out on the breastplate of integrity *and* of moral rectitude *and* right standing with God,

And having shod your feet in preparation [to face the enemy with the firm-footed stability, the promptness, and the readiness produced by the good news] of the Gospel of peace' [**Isaiah 52:7**]

Lift up over all the [covering] shield of saving faith, upon which you can quench all the flaming missiles of the wicked [one].

And take the helmet of salvation and the sword that the Spirit wields, which is the Word of God.

Pray at all times (on every occasion, in every season) in the Spirit, with all [manner of] prayer and entreaty. To that end keep alert and watch with strong purpose *and* perseverance, interceding in behalf of all the saints (God's consecrated people).

And [pray] also for me, that [freedom of] utterance may be given me, that I may open my mouth to proclaim boldly the mystery of the good news (the Gospel).

Ephesians 6:10-19 AMP

The Lord gives his people strength;
The Lord blesses his people with peace.

Psalm 29:11 HCSB

Stay alert! Watch out for your great enemy, the devil. He prowls around like a roaring lion, looking for someone to devour. Stand firm against him, and be strong in your faith. Remember that your family of believers all over the world is going through the same kind of suffering you are.

1 Peter 5:8-9 NLT

Submit yourselves therefore to God. Resist the devil, and he will flee from you.

James 4:7 KJV

Casting the whole of your care [all your anxieties, all your worries, all your concerns, once and for all] on Him, for He cares for you affectionately *and* cares about you watchfully. [Psalm 55:22.] Be well balanced (temperate, sober of mind), be viligant *and* cautious at all times; for that enemy of yours, the devil, roams around like a lion roaring [in fierce hunger], seeking someone to seize upon *and* devour. Withstand him; be firm in faith [against his onset – rooted, established, strong, immovable, and determined], knowing that the same (identical) sufferings are appointed to your brotherhood (the whole body of Christians) throughout the world.

1 Peter 5:7-9 AMP

WHO YOU ARE IN CHRIST

I will praise you because I have been remarkably and wondrously made. Your works are wondrous, and I know this very well.

Psalm 139:13-14 HCSB

For we are God's masterpiece. He has created us anew in Christ Jesus, so we can do the good things he planned for us long ago.

Ephesians 2:10 NLT

And I am convinced *and* sure of this very thing, that He Who began a good work in you will continue until the day of Jesus Christ [right up to the time of His return], developing [that good work] *and* perfecting *and* bringing it to full completion in you.

Philippians 1:6 AMP

[O] brethren beloved by God, we recognize *and* know that He has selected (chosen) you.

Thessalonians 1:4 AMP

So all of us who have had that veil removed can see and reflect the glory of the Lord. And the Lord – who is the Spirt – makes us more and more like him as we are changed into his glorious image.

Corinthians 3:18 NLT

Therefore if any person is [ingrafted] in Christ (the Messiah) (s)he is a new creation (a new creature altogether); the old [previous moral and spiritual condition] has passed away. Behold, the fresh and new has come!

2 Corinthians 5:17 AMP(s) *added*

And they have overcome (conquered) him by means of the blood of the Lamb and by the utterance of their testimony, for they did not love *and* cling to life even when faced with death [holding their lives cheap till they had to die for their witnessing.]

Revelation 12:11 AMP

Jesus said to the people who believed in him, "You are truly my disciples if your remain faithful to my teachings. And you will know the truth, and the truth will set you free.

John 8:31-32 NLT

He himself bore our sins in his body on the tree, that we might die to sin and live to righteousness. By his wounds you have been healed. For you were straying like sheep, but have now returned to the Shepherd and Overseer of your souls.

1 Peter 2:24-25 ESV

For [the Spirit which] you have now received [is] not a spirit of slavery to put you once more in bondage to fear, but you have received the Spirit of adoption [the Spirit producing sonship] in the bliss of] which we cry, Abba (Father)! Father! The Spirit Himself (thus) testifies together with our own spirit, [assuring us] that we are children of God. And if we are [His] children, then we are [His] heirs also: heirs of God and fellow heirs with Christ [sharing His inheritance with Him}; only we must share His suffering if we are to share His glory.

Romans 8:15-17 AMPC

SCRIPTURES FOR HEALING

Yet it was our weaknesses he carried; it was our sorrows that weighed him down. And we thought his troubles were a punishment from God, a punishment for his own sins! But he was pierced for our rebellion, crushed for our sins. He was beaten so we could be whole. He was whipped so we could be healed. All of us, like sheep, have strayed away. We have left God's paths to follow our own. Yet the LORD laid on him the sins of us all.

Isaiah 53:4-6 NLT

And he said to her, "Daughter, your faith has made you well. Go in peace. Your suffering is over.

Mark 5:34 NLT

Confess to one another therefore your faults (your slips, your false steps, your offenses, your sins) *and* pray [also] for one another, that you may be healed and restored [to a spiritual tone of mind and heart]. The earnest (heartfelt, continued) prayer of a righteous man makes tremendous power available [dynamic in its working].

James 5:16 AMPC

He heals the brokenhearted and binds up their wounds [curing their pains and their sorrows]. [Psalm 34:18; Isaiah 57:15; Isaiah 61:1; Luke 4:18.]

Psalm 147:3 AMPC

Cast your burden on the LORD, and he will sustain you; he will never permit the righteous to be moved.

Psalm 55:22 ESV

155

Fear not, for I *am* with you; Be not dismayed, for I *am* your God. I will strengthen you, Yes, I will help, I will uphold you with My righteous right hand.

Isaiah 41:10 NKJV

Now faith is the reality of what is hoped for, the proof of what is not seen.

Hebrews 11:1 HCSB

We are assured *and* know that [God being a partner in their labor] all things work together *and* are [fitting into a plan] for good to *and* for those who love God and are called according to [His] design *and* purpose.

Romans 8:28 AMPC

Truly, I say to you, whoever says to this mountain, 'Be taken up and thrown into the sea,' and does not doubt in his heart, but believes that what he says will come to pass, it will be done for him.

Mark 11:23 ESV

Dear friends, never take revenge. Leave that to the righteous anger of God. For the Scriptures say,

"I will take revenge;
I will pay them back,"
says the LORD.

Romans 12:19 NLT

Blessed be the God and Father of our Lord Jesus Christ, the Father of mercies and God of all comfort, who comforts us in all our affliction so that we will be able to comfort those who are in any affliction with the comfort with which we ourselves are comforted by God.

2 Corinthians 1:3-4 NASB

Danielle Cador

SPEAKING GOD'S TRUTH OVER FEARS

Have you never heard? Have you never understood? The LORD is the everlasting God, the Creator of all the earth. He never grows weak or weary. No one can measure the depths of his understanding. He gives power to the weak and strength to the powerless. Even youths will become weak and tire, and young men will fall in exhaustion. But those who trust in the LORD will find new strength. They will soar high on wings like eagles. They will run and not grow weary. They will walk and not faint.

Isaiah 40:28-31 NLT

I am sure of this, that He who started a good work in you will carry it on to completion until the day of Christ Jesus.

Philippians 1:6 HCSB

I do not consider, brethren, that I have captured *and* made it my own [yet]; but one thing I do [it is my one aspiration]; forgetting what lies behind and straining forward to what lies ahead, I press on toward the goal to win the [supreme and heavenly] prize to which God in Christ Jesus is calling us upward.

Philippians 3:13-14 AMPC

I can do all things through Christ who strengthens me.

Philippians 4:13 NKJV

Jesus Christ (the Messiah) is [always] the same, yesterday, today, [yes] and forever (to the ages).

Hebrews 13:8 AMPC

God will do this, for he is faithful to do what he says, and he has invited you into partnership with his Son, Jesus Christ our Lord.

1 Corinthians 1:9 NLT

God will wipe away every tear from their eyes; and death shall be no more, neither shall there be anguish (sorrow and mourning) nor grief nor pain any more, for the old conditions *and* the former order of things have passed away. [Isaiah 25:8; 35:10.]

Revelation 21:4 AMPC

When I am afraid,
I will trust in You.

Psalm 56:3 HCSB

He who planted the ear, shall He not hear? He formed the eye, shall He not see?

Psalm 94:9 NKJV

Do not be conformed to this world, but be transformed by the renewal of your mind, that by testing you may discern what is the will of God, what is good and acceptable and perfect.

Romans 12:2 ESV

Since you have been raised to new life with Christ, set your sights on the realities of heaven, where Christ sits in the place of honor at God's right hand. Think about the things of heaven, not the things of earth.

Colossians 3:1-2 NLT

For God did not give us a spirit of timidity (of cowardice, of craven and cringing and fawning fear), but [He has given us a spirit of power and of love and of calm *and* well-balanced mind *and* discipline *and* self-control.

2 Timothy 1:7 AMPC

Danielle Cador

The earth and everything in it,
The world and its inhabitants,
Belong to the LORD;

Psalm 24:1 HCSB

Oh, how great *is* Your goodness,
Which You have laid up for those who
fear You,
Which You have prepared for those who
trust in You
In the presence of the sons of men!

Psalm 31:19 NKJV

For every beast of the forest is mine,
the cattle on a thousand hills.
I know all the birds of the hills,
And all that moves in the field is mine.

Psalm 50:10-11 ESV

That is why I tell you not to worry about everyday life—whether you
have enough food and drink, or enough clothes to wear. Isn't life more
than food, and your body more than clothing? Look at the birds. They
don't plant or harvest or store food in barns, for your heavenly Father
feeds them. And aren't you far more valuable to him than they are? Can
all your worries add a single moment to your life? And why worry about
your clothing? Look at the lilies of the field and how they grow. They
don't work or make their clothing, yet Solomon in all his glory was not
dressed as beautifully as they are. And if God cares so wonderfully for
wildflowers that are here today and thrown into the fire tomorrow, he
will certainly care for you. Why do you have so little faith? So don't
worry about these things, saying 'What will we eat? What will we drink?
What will we wear?' These things dominate the thoughts of unbelievers,
but your heavenly Father already knows all your needs. Seek the
Kingdom of God above all else, and live righteously, and he will give
you everything you need.

Matthew 6:25-33 NLT

Now to Him Who, by (in consequence of) the [action of His] power that is at work within us, is able to [carry out His purpose and] do superabundantly, far over *and* above all that we [dare] ask or think [infinitely beyond our highest prayers, desires, thoughts, hopes, or dreams].

Ephesians 3:20 AMPC

Danielle Cador

WALKING IN FAITH

For it is by free grace (God's unmerited favor) that you are saved (delivered from judgment *and* made partakers of Christ's salvation) through [your] faith. And this [salvation] is not of yourselves [of your own doing, it came not through your own striving], but it is the gift of God.

Ephesians 2:8 AMPC

Faith shows the reality of what we hope for; it is the evidence of things we cannot see.

Hebrews 11:1 NLT

But without faith *it is* impossible to please *Him*, for he who comes to God must believe that He is, and *that* He is a rewarded of those who diligently seek Him.

Hebrews 11:6 NKJV

For God so greatly loved *and* dearly prized the world that He [even] gave up His only begotten (unique) Son, so that whoever believes in (trusts in, clings to, relies on) Him shall not perish (come to destruction, be lost) but have eternal (everlasting) life.

John 3:16 AMPC

And Jesus answered them, "Truly, I say to you, if you have faith and do not doubt, you will not only do what has been done to the fig tree, but even if you say to this mountain, 'Be taken up and thrown into the sea,' it will happen."

Matthew 21:21 ESV

Holding fast to faith (that leaning of the entire human personality on God in absolute trust and confidence) and having a good (clear) conscience. By rejecting *and* thrusting from them [their conscience], some individuals have made shipwreck of their faith.

1 Timothy 1:19 AMPC

So all who put their faith in Christ share the same blessing Abraham received because of his faith.

Galatians 3:9 NLT

Dear brothers and sisters, when troubles of any kind come your way, consider it an opportunity for great joy. For you know that when your faith is tested, your endurance has a chance to grow. So let grow, for when your endurance is fully developed, you will be perfect and complete, needing nothing.

James 1:2-4 NLT

So that [the genuineness] of your faith may be tested, [your faith] which is infinitely more precious than the perishable gold which is tested *and* purified by fire. [This proving of your faith is intended] to redound to [your] praise and glory and honor when Jesus Christ (the Messiah, the Anointed One) is revealed.

1 Peter 1:7 AMPC

ACKNOWLEDGMENTS

I know that this is the section where one thanks every person that has played a part in getting the book together, but, in all honesty, the Holy Spirit really pushed me in completing this book. The times I wanted to give up, primarily due to fear, were not an option. The Holy Spirit tapped into some of my friends, who would send me 'random' texts asking how my book was coming. That's when I truly realized the importance of this book. The importance of strongholds and chains being broken in the name of Jesus. Healing taking place. Forgiveness taking place. Transformation taking place. God was going to make sure this book was completed. I do thank my friends who encouraged me by sharing their excitement about my first book being published. And, I have to thank God for my story. Not one I would've imagined, at all. But, I am thankful for it. Thankful for how it showed me how much I need God, and that He was always with me, and will continue to be with me. My story just makes my journey that much stronger, and more dependent on His strength. The journey's just beginning, and I thank you for being a part of it.

Danielle Cador

www.ingramcontent.com/pod-product-compliance
Lightning Source LLC
Chambersburg PA
CBHW070344100426
42812CB00005B/1418